Coaching Girls' Ice Hockey

Dr. Gerald A. Walford
and
Gerald E. Walford

Wish Publishing
Terre Haute, Indiana
www.wishpublishing.com

LCCN: 2003101480

Proofread by Heather Lowhorn
Edited by Christopher Stolle
Cover designed by Phil Velikan
Cover photo by www.painetworks.com
Interior diagrams by Debbie Oldenburg; illustrations by Phil Velikan
Section opening graphics by www.RebelArtist.com

Printed in the United States of America
10 9 8 7 6 5 4 3 2 1

Published in the United States by
Wish Publishing
P.O. Box 10337
Terre Haute, IN 47801, USA
www.wishpublishing.com

Distributed in the United States by
Cardinal Publishers Group
7301 Georgetown Road, Suite 118
Indianapolis, Indiana 46268
www.cardinalpub.com

Table of Contents

Introduction

Realize your potential. Create your potential. Play to your potential.

Sports and recreation are becoming not only physical games but also mental games. The two must go together. This book combines the physical and mental aspects for the coach and the players. Coaches must understand the mental problems of the athletes and the athletes must understand the coach's plans. To help with the mental game the martial arts, Eastern philosophy, NLF (Neurolinguistic Programming), Western philosophy and zen are promoted.

Physical skill must be learned and then executed under pressure situations. Pressure control is the essence of sports. A skill or strategy is of no use unless it will hold up under pressure. This is where mind control is needed. The mind controls the body.

Learning is the responsibility of the player and the coach. The player is responsible for her learning. The coach can help. Teammates can help. Others may help. Ultimately it is the responsibility of the player. No one can make you better. They can help you make yourself better, but the motivation is your responsibility. It is your time, effort and dedication.

Golfers hit balls by the hour. Basketball players shoot hoops by the hours. Baseball pitchers throw balls by the hours. High jumpers jump, skiers race, etc. Hockey players must also practice by the hours. Skills must be learned so well that they will be performed automatically. So automatic that no thinking is needed.

Learning is fun. Practice can be fun. Have fun. Enjoy the experience.

Gerry A. Walford and Gerry E. Walford

Section 1:
Individual Skills

I ndividual skills — or fundamentals — are the basis of the game. Team strategy is of no value if the play ers cannot perform the skills of passing, shooting, puck control, etc. A team that cannot pass to each other cannot attack. A team that cannot use agility skating to cover its opponent cannot defend its goal. Individual skills must be mastered.

Chapter One:
Skating

Skating is the basis of offensive and defensive hockey. Goaltenders require excellent skating and agility techniques. The better the skating skills, the easier it is to perform the puck control, shooting and team strategies. There are two main styles of skating: forward and backward. Each style has its freestyle and agility-style requirements.

Beginners have difficulty skating because they try to skate like they walk. This cannot be done. Look at figures 1-1 and 1-2. In the running action of 1-1, notice

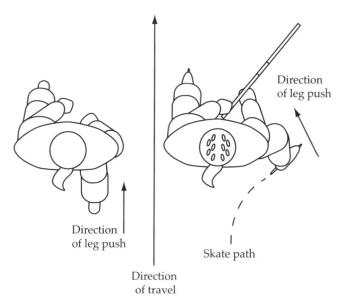

Figure 1-1: Running Action   Figure 1-2: Skating Action

how the leg pushes in the direction of travel. The skater's basic push is to the side and away from the body (diag. 1-2).

In walking or running, the leg moves forward, touches the ground under the body's center of gravity and then pushes straight back in the direction of travel.

In skating, the leg moves under the body's center of gravity and glides forward, with the toe pointing in the direction of travel. The knee then leads the leg and foot in rotating outward and pushing away from the direction of travel. As the leg extends to almost maximum extension, the pushing action is completed and the leg swings back around behind the body to repeat the glide action (diag. 1-3).

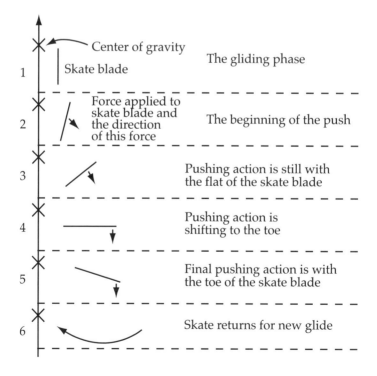

Figure 1-3: The Skating Phase

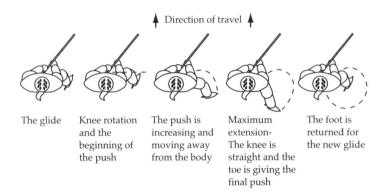

The glide | Knee rotation and the beginning of the push | The push is increasing and moving away from the body | Maximum extension-The knee is straight and the toe is giving the final push | The foot is returned for the new glide

Figure 1-4: Circular Leg Action

Stand behind a runner as she runs away from you. Notice how the legs move in a straight line. Stand behind a skater and you will notice how the legs move in a circular pattern (figure 1-4).

The arm and shoulder movement in skating and running is also different. When the runner's right leg is forward, the left arm and shoulder are forward. In freestyle skating, the right arm and shoulder are forward, with the right leg forward. However, in skating, especially with puck control, there is minimal shoulder action. When running, both legs are often off the ground at a certain time. In skating, one leg is always in contact with the ice. Since the leg thrust is to the side of the direction of travel, the other foot has to be in contact with the ice to steer the body in its direction. This is much like a sailboat using the keel and rudder of the ship to steer the ship when the wind is hitting the side of the ship.

FORWARD SKATING

The head maintains an upright position. The head does not bob, drop or shake, despite the strong movements from the lower body and legs. The head is up and rotates to look and evaluate various situations.

Watch a good skater from the side view and you will notice how the head moves along level with the ice.

Body lean is determined by speed and/or acceleration. More speed, more lean. The body lean must not be excessive, or the leg thrust will not be through the body and the body's center of gravity. Notice in figure 1-5 how the leg thrust is directed through the body and up into the head. Thrusting above or below the bodyline will give a weak and powerless thrust.

Figure 1-5: Direction of Thrust

Hips and upper thighs provide the power to the thrust through a three-phase action.

The recovery phase: After the final thrust, the skate breaks contact with the ice and swings around behind the body for the glide.

The gliding phase: The skate swings around under the body and contacts the ice — for gliding action and to support the body weight.

The pushing or thrusting phase: From the gliding action, the leg is rotated outward as in figures 1-2 and 1-3 to give the movement forward.

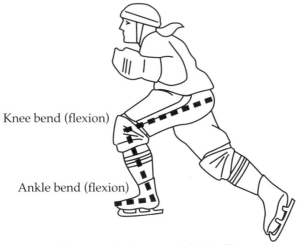

Knee bend (flexion)

Ankle bend (flexion)

Figure 1-6: Knee and Ankle Flex

In the gliding phase, the knee and ankle are well-bent. The ankle is bent toward the knee. This ankle bend is very important. If the bend is insufficient, the lower leg (from the ankle to the knee) is too upright and the body cannot achieve proper balance, as the body is back on the heels too much. Beginners often have difficulty achieving balance, as they are forced into too much of an upright posture because their skates are too stiff and prevent the proper ankle bend forward. They are told to bend their knees, but they can't because of the lack of ankle bend. The Russians had an effective solution for this problem. They simply did not lace their skates all the way up to the top. They left the top one or two eyelets open. Lack of knee and ankle bend also prevents a powerful leg thrust, as the faster the leg is thrust from the bent position to the straight position, the faster the body is propelled forward.

BACKWARD SKATING

Backward skating is a demanding skill. The initial stages of learning are often difficult, but practice will make it natural and easy. Backward skating is required for defensewomen, as it is totally necessary for the position. Forwards are usually weak in this area, as they do not use it as much as the defensewomen.

Again, the head is erect and not drooped forward. The head must remain up so that the head can be rotated to either side for analysis of the situation. Poor backward skaters often droop or drop their head to the chest in an attempt to maintain balance. When this is done, the player must lift her head and shoulders to look around. This often puts her *off balance* for immediate action. The action is delayed.

In backward skating, the upper body action should be minimal. Excessive arm swinging and shoulder action to build up speed are detrimental to immediate agility action. The player must learn good leg thrusts and balance.

The key to the leg thrust is to achieve inward knee rotation, along with good knee and ankle flexion. Such leg positioning will give a strong thrust backward. Very often, players will use a wide arc pushing action with the leg. This is not desirable, as the short arc with a strong thrust puts the body in line with the direction of travel. The wide arc push gives too much sway to the body and is less efficient. Wide arc backward skaters are unable to lift their skates off the ice, as both skates are always in contact with the ice for balance. This wide arc prevents quick agility movement. As in forward skating, one leg is gliding and the other is thrusting. Good backward skaters are able to build up speed from a backward position. Poor backward skaters often have to skate forward to build up momentum and speed, then pivot to backward skating. An attacker can take advantage of this folly.

THE PIVOT

The pivot is used to go from forward to backward skating and from backward skating to forward skating. Many players are weak in this area, as they simply twist their feet on the ice as their body is spinning. This is dangerous, as an imperfection in the ice can catch the skate blade and trip the player.

Backward to Forward Pivot

Figure 1-7 shows this quite nicely.

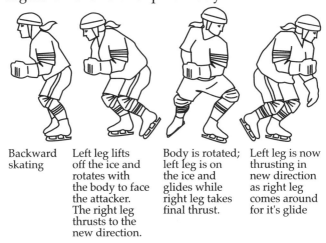

| Backward skating | Left leg lifts off the ice and rotates with the body to face the attacker. The right leg thrusts to the new direction. | Body is rotated; left leg is on the ice and glides while right leg takes final thrust. | Left leg is now thrusting in new direction as right leg comes around for it's glide |

Figure 1-7: Backward to Forward Skating

Forward to Backward Skating

Again, there is no crossover of the legs. While gliding forward on one leg, the other leg is lifted off the ice and swings around to point at the toe of the gliding leg. The body swings around so that the lifted leg now drops to the ice and becomes the gliding leg as the other leg swings around to continue in the backward skating action (diag. 1-8).

THE CROSSOVER

Skaters often use the crossover of the legs to change directions. The player makes a two-legged stop and the outside leg (the leg away from the body lean or new direction of travel) is lifted up and crossed over in front

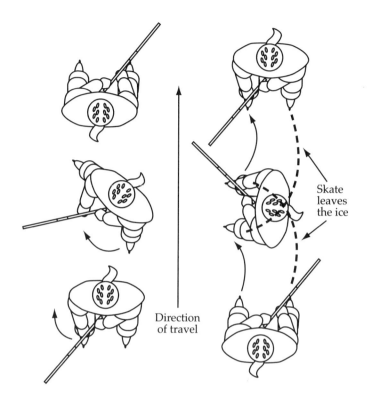

Figure 1-8: Backward to Forward/Forward to Backward

of the body as the body turns in the new direction. This action is not desirable for several reasons:

1. As the leg is crossing over, the player can be easily knocked off-balance.

2. Once the leg begins the crossover, the player is committed to this direction and cannot make a quick adjustment to move in another direction to cover an attacker or for a passing adjustment.

3. When crossing over, the inside leg is straight, the body is lifted up and the body leans in the new direction. The player is vulnerable, off-balance and in a weak position. Athletes in other sports do not use the crossover.

The crossover should be eliminated, and the correct stop and change of direction is explained as follows.

STOPS AND CHANGE OF DIRECTIONS

To stop, the player must put her skate blades at right angles to the direction of travel. If possible, it is best to use both blades, as the stop is quicker and more powerful than the one-leg stop. The body must shift or turn with the feet or even ahead of the feet. The body shift must not be later than the turning of the feet. The knees and ankles must provide good flexion to absorb the shock, balance and stability. This bending of the knees and ankles puts the body in position for a change of direction.

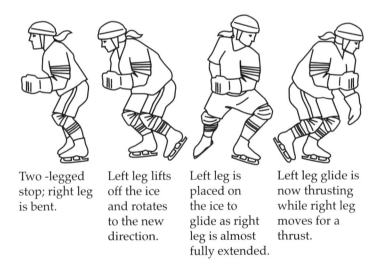

Two-legged stop; right leg is bent.

Left leg lifts off the ice and rotates to the new direction.

Left leg is placed on the ice to glide as right leg is almost fully extended.

Left leg glide is now thrusting while right leg moves for a thrust.

Figure 1-9: Stop and Go

The mechanics for stopping and starting are similar to the backward-to-forward pivot. There is no crossing over of the legs. In the stop, the outside leg must have a good bend. As the stop is almost complete, body weight shifts to the outside leg as the inside leg lifts and rotates to the new direction of travel. The outside leg — being fully flexed from the stopping action — is ready to thrust in the new direction.

Now, if there is a change in the situation and the player cannot move in the new direction, the body is still balanced. The inside leg that was lifted can now be placed on the ice and the body can now move to the new direction. This skill is especially valuable when covering an attacker or moving in congested areas.

SCOOTING

This skating action is similar to riding on a scooter. One leg glides and the other leg does the thrusting. In close quarters and along the boards, this skill can be quite valuable.

Chapter Two:
Puck Control

Puck control involves the skills of stickhandling, passing, pass receiving and shooting. Puck control organizes and controls the game. Strategy is based on puck control. Control the puck and you control the game.

THE HOCKEY STICK

The hockey stick is a very individual choice. It seems that the best method for stick selection is trial and error. Play and experiment with the various lengths, shaft flexes and lies.

STICKHANDLING

Stickhandling is controlling the puck while moving in open ice and in congested areas. Good stickhandlers set up the play. They are the playmakers and are vital to strategy. Stickhandling is like giving and receiving your own passes. The puck is feathered and not banged or slapped back and forth. The puck is moved from side to side and front to side. The skill must be performed with the arms free from the body and not jammed into the sides or jammed into the front of the body. With this freedom, the arms are able to move around the body with relative ease.

The puck is controlled by feel, not by sight. The eyes are needed for looking around and evaluating the situation. Players are often able to perform this skill while looking at the puck but lack the confidence to look up and around. They have a fear of losing the puck. Coaches must recognize this and encourage the player to keep trying, even though the puck might occasionally be lost. Coaches must offer drills and encouragement to promote this skill. Coaches must also help the players who are able to stickhandle with the head and eyes up during practice but fail in game or pressure situations.

PASSING

When passing, the passer must push the stick toward the target. The blade of the stick should be at right angles to the target. Figures 2-1 and 2-2 show these requirements.

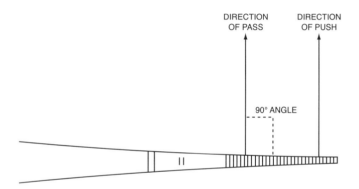

Figure 2-1: Direction of the Pass

In the incorrect figure (2-2), the point of release must be precise. If the point of release is too far forward or backward, the pass will miss the target. By pushing the blade and puck in line toward the target, it is much easier to get accurate direction. Good passers move the whole stick, not just the blade, toward the target. This is accomplished by moving the top hand toward the target along with the bottom hand. Poor passers tend to let the top hand jamb into the body. This causes the stick to swing around in an arc instead of straight at the target.

The pass is released from the blade of the stick while the shaft is perpendicular to the ice or leaning slightly

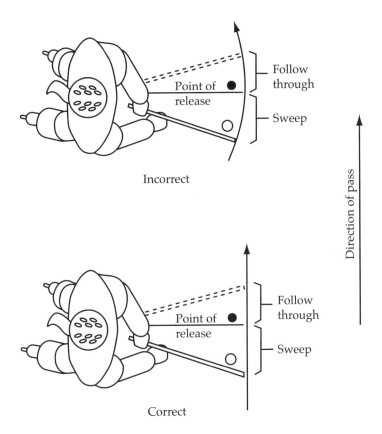

Incorrect

Direction of pass

Correct

Sweep pass   Path taken by blade of hockey stick

Figure 2-2: Pass Release

forward over the puck. Do not release the puck when the shaft is leaning away from the puck, as this gives a weak pass and usually a lifting of the puck off the ice. During the passing action, the body must stay in balance and not fall backward from the arm's forward movement.

THE SWEEP PASS

This is the basic pass. The blade of the stick sweeps the puck from in back of the body, forward to the release point (figure 2-3).

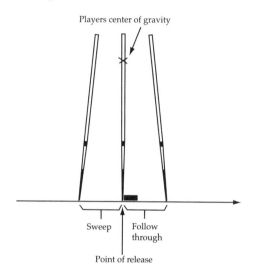

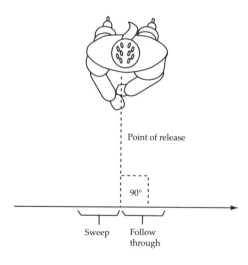

Figure 2-3: Point of Release

THE SLAP PASS

This is similar to the sweep pass except the sweeping action is off the ice and makes contact with the puck just prior to release.

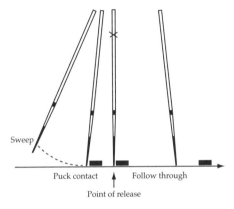

Figure 2-4: The Slap Pass

THE SNAP PASS

The snap pass is like the slap pass except the sweep and follow-through are very short but powerful.

THE LIFT (OR FLIP) PASS

The lift pass is needed to lift the puck over obstacles. The release is later than in the other passes.

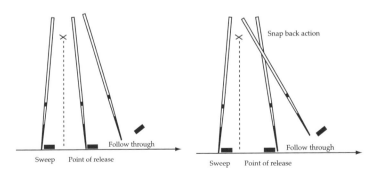

Figure 2-5: The Lift Pass

THE BACKHAND PASS

A player must be able to make all the passes in a forehand or backhand manner. The skills are the same as the forehand passes except the bottom hand pulls the stick rather than pushes the stick, as in the forehand pass.

THE DROP PASS AND BACK PASS

As the player is skating forward, the puck is moved to the side of the body and the blade of the stick is placed in front of the puck to stop its forward progression. This must be executed so that the puck remains stationary, not moving. The back pass is similar, but the blade of the stick pulls the puck back so that the puck is sliding back instead of forward.

Accurate passes are easier if the pass receiver has her stick blade on the ice to give the passer a target. This way, the passer knows where the receiver wants the puck. The passer does not have to guess where to put the puck for the receiver.

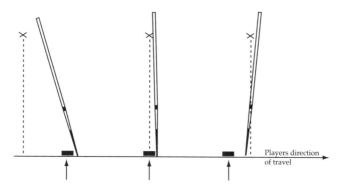

Players direction of travel

Figure 2-6: Drop Pass

The passer must know when to pass. Blind passes are dangerous, unless the passer knows for sure the receiver is in position. This knowledge usually takes time with lots of experience with each other.

PASS RECEIVING

A pass is of no value if the player cannot receive the pass. The pass receiver should place the blade of the stick on the ice where she wants to receive the puck. This gives the passer a target. The blade of the stick should be square to the pass and leaning slightly over the puck to prevent the puck from bouncing over the blade. In most cases, especially with fast passes, the pass receiver provides a cushion for the puck by letting the stick have a little give on impact.

Sometimes, the pass receiver has to adjust to receive a poor pass. These adjustments might take the form of speeding up or slowing down. For passes into the feet, the receiver has to learn how to direct the puck forward in front of her by using her feet. Care must be taken when looking at the feet, as the receiver might be vulnerable for a body check.

SHOOTING

Skating and passing put the puck into scoring position. The shot must be good. Scoring opportunities are limited, so players must be able to take advantage when the opportunities arise.

The mechanics of shooting are very similar to passing. The body is over the puck and in balance. At impact, the player's weight is over the front leg. The body does not fall backward from the shot.

THE SWEEP (OR WRIST) SHOT

This is similar to the sweep pass. The puck is well back from the body. The weight is on the forward, or gliding, leg. The blade of the stick is cupped over the puck as the puck is swept forward along the ice to the point of release. During the sweep, the stick's shaft pushes downward and forward to bend the shaft. At the point of release, the wrists can give a extra snap. A low follow-through means a low shot, and a high follow-through means a high shot. The extra wrist snap also helps in the height of the shot.

A problem with weak shooters is that they often try to shoot the puck when the puck is too far in front of the body. There is no power to this shot, as the shooter is unable to press the shaft into the ice for the shot.

Although this is the basic shot, the shooter should learn to shoot in stride and off either foot. By shooting in stride, the goaltender has difficulty in reading when the shot is coming. Most shooters glide or stop some movements in preparation for the shot. This is the clue to the goaltender to prepare for the shot. Shooting in stride gives no forewarning to the goaltender.

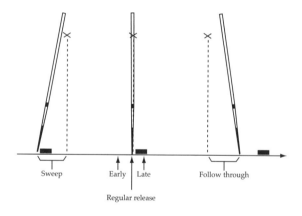

Figure 2-7: The Sweep Pass

THE SLAP SHOT

In the sweep shot, the puck is in contact with the blade for the sweep. In the slap shot, the blade of the stick is off the ice for the shot and makes contact with the puck just prior to release of the puck. On the downswing, the stick is forced down into the ice and through the puck. The slap shot can be accurate if it is practiced for accuracy. Most practice the shot for power. Accuracy and power can be achieved with practice. Some have found it helpful to take a shorter backswing for

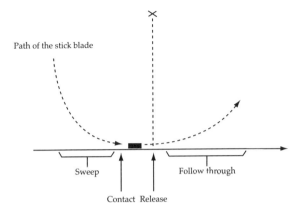

Figure 2-8: Slap Shot

the slap shot. Another advantage of the shorter backswing is that the shot is executed quicker to the goal. The goaltender has less time to read the shot and know when it's coming. Puck placement can determine the height of the shot. If the puck is back, the shot is low. If the puck is forward, the shot is high.

THE FLIP SHOT

This is the same as the flip pass. This shot can be dangerous to the goaltender if the puck bounces in front of the goaltender, as the bounce can be very unpredictable.

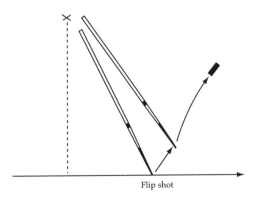

Figure 2-9: The Flip Shot

THE BACKHAND SHOT

This shot is difficult for the goaltender to read and, as a result, should be used more often. The mechanics for the backhand are similar to the forehand shot except the low hand pulls instead of pushes.

The shooting mechanics outlined are for the basic shot. Good players learn and practice to shoot even when the body is not in the correct position or in balance.

Some players prefer to shoot off the heel of the blade, while others like to shoot off the toe or middle of the blade. Experiment to find your preference, but learn to shoot off all positions from the heel to the toe.

ACHIEVING POWER IN PASSING AND SHOOTING

Power is achieved by three factors:
1. Downward force
2. Length of sweep
3. Speed of the hands and arms

Downward force

When the stick is forced into the ice, the shaft bends to the amount of force used. This bend forces the blade to lag behind the hands and upper part of the stick. As the stick moves forward, the lag increases, and at the point of release, the blade springs forward to catch up with the rest of the stick. This catch-up speed adds power to the speed of the hands. The stiffness of the shaft varies with the individual. Strong players are able to get good bend to a stiff shaft, which gives faster catch-up speed. Some shafts are too stiff for some players, so they will perform better with a lesser stiff shaft. The more bend, the more catch-up distance. The stiffer the shaft, the faster the catch-up speed. Too whippy a shaft will give lots of catch-up distance but poor catch-up speed. The player must experiment to find the correct shaft flex for her.

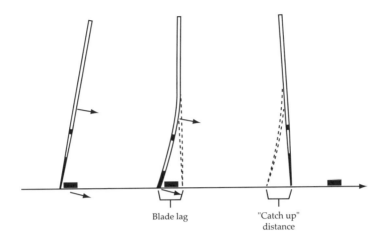

Blade lag   "Catch up"
                  distance

Figure 2-10: Downward Force

Length of Sweep

The longer the sweep, the greater momentum built up prior to release of the puck. This is true to a certain extent, as too long a backswing might be cumbersome and inefficient in some game situations.

Speed of the Hands and Arms

The faster the hands and arms move into and through the shot, the faster the shot. Powerful shooters are able to maximize all three factors.

DEKING AND BEATING AN OPPONENT WHILE STICKHANDLING

Deceiving or beating an opponent is often called a deke or throwing a deke. The deke is simply a trick or deception to make the opponent think you are going to do something you are not going to do. Such deception requires excellent skating and puck control. Timing of the action is crucial to execution, so the player must practice the following skills intensively.

Various body moves can be made to look as if the puck carrier is going to go one way and then change directions. The shoulder can drop and/or a slight body twist can deceive an opponent. Once the opponent makes a commitment, then the puck carrier can change directions. Deception can be done with a leg crossing over for a fake change of directions. A weaving of the body or a zigzag pattern can be deceptive. Some players wait until the last split second and then just jump to the side or just slip the body sideways in a draw-away action. A change of pace is highly effective. Some have executed the change of pace by moving the legs fast but not letting the legs rotate for a strong thrust. By not rotating the legs for the strong thrust, the skate points straight ahead and the feet slide quickly over the ice by not digging in. One variation to the change of pace is to use a fast break or the stop and go. A fake pass and or a fake shot can also be effective.

Players must learn to use various tricks and not become stereotyped in their moves. Some players can only move effectively to one side. These players soon become ineffective, as the opposition knows their moves.

Chapter Three: Goaltending

Goaltending might well be the most demanding position on the team. In fact, this might be the position to place your best athlete, if she has the courage. With all the heavy protective equipment, the goaltender must be able to have excellent agility, reflexes, eyesight and courage. Good goaltenders have a hockey sense as to the play around them and when the shot will come. They have this anticipation of the play. With experience, they develop the ability to read the shot by the body and stick manipulation of the shooter.

THE STANCE

The goaltender must have a stance that will provide explosive action in all directions. Naturally, balance is the main requirement. An imperfection in the balance and stance will cause a slight delay in movement. Such delays might mean a goal. The proper stance is a spreading of the feet and a squatting with the legs so that the body's center of gravity is between the skate blades. Trial and error through experimentation will determine the spread of the feet for best movement in all directions. The amount of knee bend for the squatting action is also determined by trial and error. The squat must maintain a solid base so that the body is balanced over the skate blades. This action requires good hip, knee and ankle flexion (figure 3-1). Notice in A and B how the body is centered with body weight evenly balanced. In C and D the weight is unevenly distributed.

The upper body should lean forward, with the arms

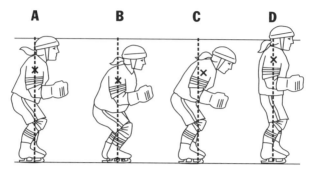

Figure 3-1: The Stance

hanging but in a ready position for quick action. The spine should be relatively straight, not hunched over. The head should be held high for good visibility. This stance will give the goaltender good breathing action. Many goaltenders knock the knees slightly into each other so that they have the legs ready for thrusting to either side. The stick hand should hold the goal stick flat on the ice while the catching hand is open and facing the shot. The goal stick should be slightly in front of the feet so that a shot on the goal stick will have some cushion space to help absorb some of the shot's power. If the stick is too tight to the feet, the puck can rebound off the stick and end up in a dangerous place for another shot on goal.

LATERAL MOVEMENT

Quick lateral movement is essential to defending the goal. Shooters are not going to aim at the body, so the goaltender must move to either side for the shot. The lateral move is relatively simple. The thrusting leg bends in at the knee if the knee is not already in this position from the stance. The leg thrusts while the other leg rotates outward to provide a gliding action. Sometimes, the gliding leg is lifted off the ice. To stop — or to stop and change directions — the gliding leg makes a stopping action. To change directions, just thrust with the stopping leg while the other leg becomes the gliding leg. Good goaltenders drill constantly at the stopping and starting in the other direction. This is a basic skill to goaltending. The quicker the move, the better the chance of stopping the puck (figure 3-2). This lateral move is also to move from one goal post to the other.

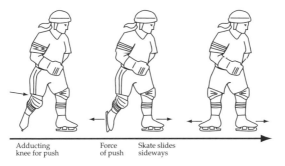

Adducting   Force   Skate slides
knee for push   of push   sideways

Figure 3-2: The Lateral Move

Backward skating is essential to goaltending. Goaltenders will use backward skating to move from one post to the other as well as moving back into the goal as the attack comes closer to the net. Goaltenders must learn net orientation. The goaltender has to look at the puck and yet be able to position herself to either post, without looking for the goal posts (figure 3-3).

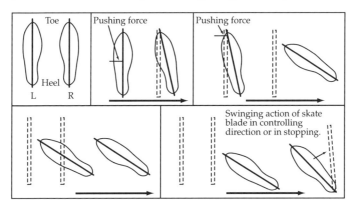

Figure 3-3

THE SIDE KICK

The side kick is throwing the leg out at the puck at the side of the body. The action is similar to the lateral move, only the gliding leg lifts and moves to the puck while the other leg thrusts. The upper body remains straight to help maintain balance and be in position for any follow-up moves. Some goaltenders fall backward on this move. This is not recommended, as the body is out of position for any future moves. The goaltender becomes down and out.

THE ONE-KNEE SLIDE

This move is the lateral move with the thrusting leg dropping to the ice as the body slides. The dropped leg gives more protection to shots along the ice. The upper body maintains an erect posture. Goaltenders practice side-to-side, one-knee slides often.

THE GLOVE HAND

The skill of catching a puck is similar to catching a ball. The glove hand should be held low, as it is easier to lift the hand for higher shots than to drop the hand for low shots. On catching the puck, be careful to not flip the hand to the chest or other areas. This flipping action might just loosen the puck and flip it into the goal.

THE BLOCKING HAND

The blocking hand has a much larger area than the catching glove and is excellent for deflecting shots. Care must be taken to deflect the shot to the proper direction. Bad deflections might mean another shot on goal. Since the blocker hand is holding the stick, the goaltender must practice moving the stick back and forth and to either side with the blade, constantly maintaining its flat position on the ice.

THE LEGS

The legs move the goal pads into various positions. Strong legs are essential. The pads must become a part of the body. Like the blocker, the goal pads should be able to deflect the puck to a desired direction or provide a cushion so that the puck drops straight down to be covered up.

THE BODY

The body is used to block shots, much like a large blocking glove or goal pads. The body should be moved to be behind the shot. The body is the main line of defense and is used to cut down the angles of shots. The glove, stick and blocker might look spectacular in their moves, but it is the body that provides the best protection to the goal. The body positioned in the correct place gives the shooter little open net to shoot for.

GOAL NET ORIENTATION

Goaltenders must be able to know exactly where the net is when they look at the puck. They must be able to move out from the goal, move side to side and back into the goal and still maintain their body position of centering a line from the puck to the center of the net. The lines on the ice and on the boards can help with the goaltenders' orientation of the net. Orientation of the net takes constant practice. Goaltenders can practice moving around by playing imaginary shots and checking to make sure they are in the correct position to block the shot. Coaches can help in these practice sessions by calling out commands like left, right, forward, back to the left post, etc.

Throughout these drills, the player must not look for the goal. The catching glove, the blocking pad and the top of the goal stick can help by swinging back to feel for the net's post. When playing in an unfamiliar rink, the goaltender should study the lines on the ice and boards, in case there is a little difference than from their home rink. The goaltender should then practice moving around to imaginary shots to get the feel of where the net is and how to move around the area. A goaltender cannot work too much on the skill of net orientation.

POSITIONAL PLAY AND PLAYING THE ANGLE

Playing the angle means that if a line is drawn from the puck to the center of the goal, the goaltender is able to bisect this line with her body. Also, it means being able to move out from the goal to block more of the net. Figure 3-4 shows how moving out on the shot line blocks more of the goal. A goaltender that stays in the net gives the shooter more open net to the sides of her body. By moving out to the puck, the shooter has less open net to each side of the body.

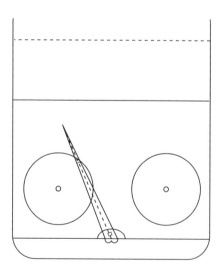

Figure 3-4

A goaltender must decide on how far to move out. She can move out far enough to block the goal area completely, but this might be extremely dangerous, as she cannot get back into the net fast enough if the puck is passed or the shot angle changes. Experience will help the goaltender to learn how far to move out and when to stay back. Coaches can help in this development with game-condition drills.

Goaltenders must constantly practice playing the angles and net orientation. It might not be easy, and it is time-consuming, but it is the basis of goaltending. Fast hands and a blocking glove will not make up for bad net orientation and/or poor angle positioning.

GENERAL RULES

The goaltender must focus on the puck but also be aware of the positional play of the other attackers. She must learn to read the developing play. Is the opponent going to shoot or pass? What is the best position to play for the shot and possible pass? The movement of the player's body and hockey stick will give clues as to whether there will be a shot or a pass. Opponents often give signals like dropping the shoulder, arm movement, lifting the leg, dropping the head, changing the skating stride, etc. The goaltender must be alert for these moves and yet not fall victim to these moves being a fake or deception.

Goaltenders should remain in a stand-up position as much as possible. The stand-up position gives the goaltender the best blocking ability for the net and being in position for a change in moves. When it is necessary for the goaltender to go down, it is best to do this by dropping to one knee. This increases a good blocking area and enhances a good recovery for standing back up or any other move that is necessary. The one-knee drop gives good balance and quick recovery, if needed. Some goaltenders do the two-knee drop, which is satisfactory if no further move is needed. The two-knee drop makes recovery very difficult as well as puts a goaltender out of position for rebounds.

It should be remembered that every move a goaltender makes should leave her in position for a recovery move. Goaltenders that flop, drop and sprawl might make the initial save but are often out of position and vulnerable for the rebound.

Goaltenders' skates must be sharp enough to give good starting and stopping action. Some goaltenders prefer sharp but not too sharp skates. Individual trial and error will decide. Dull skates will slide too much for the stopping and starting action.

Goaltenders must learn to play the puck with their goal sticks. Good goaltenders are able to pass the puck and even shoot the puck to set up plays from their own end. They are able to go behind the net and into the corners to set up a quick breakout play. This is excellent strategy, as it can quickly get the puck out of their end. A good pass by the goaltender can catch the attackers disorganized.

A goaltender must be extremely alert when the opposition has control of the puck behind her net. She must also maintain sight of the puck and the attacking players in front of the net. This is where good lateral movement is needed, as the goaltender must move from post to post depending on the movement of the puck behind the net.

When clearing or deflecting the puck, the goaltender should try to deflect the shot away from the attacking player. This helps to prevent the shooter from picking up her own rebound. If possible, clear or deflect the puck to a teammate.

In scramble situations around the goal, teammates should be careful in falling on or around the goaltender to cover the puck. Such action restricts the movement of the goaltender and sometimes even loosens the puck away from the goaltender. Instead of falling on the goaltender, the player should fall behind the goaltender as another body to protect the net.

Teammates, especially defensewomen, must be careful when backing up toward the goal. The defensewomen should back up slightly to the side of the attacker so that the goaltender can see the puck and not have her sightline to the puck blocked. It is difficult to play the shot if the goaltender is screened by her own teammate. This same rule should apply when defensewomen try to stop the shot on goal. Such action blocks the goaltender's vision. Often, if the defensewoman does not stop the shot, it is deflected into the goal.

Goaltenders should help their teammates by yelling comments like "Man behind you," "Far wing open" or "Move, you're blocking my vision."

Goaltenders can often be in position to receive a pass from a teammate and provide a relay to a far wing. This is highly effective.

GOALTENDER DRILLS

Post to post: The goaltender stands at one post and moves to the other post and back and forth as fast as possible with the body staying erect.

Front of net and back to goal posts: The goaltender stands in front of the net and moves back to the right goal post and then moves back out to the center and then back to the left goal post. The body must face straight ahead at all times.

The leg kick: The goaltender practices alternating leg kicks to each side while remaining in balance for the next move.

The one-knee slide: The goaltender stands at one goal post and slides to the other goal post with the one-knee drop, then stands up and repeats back to the original position.

Mirror drill: The goaltender mirrors the movements of the coach or the other goaltender. Each goaltender takes turns as the leader.

These drills are excellent conditioning drills, especially for interval training.

Stationary shots: Players line up across the rink in front of the goaltender and shoot at the goaltender. It is best to have the shots alternate from the right and left sides so that the goaltender has to move to cover the angles.

Various angles: Have the players attack the net from various angles so that the goaltender can work on her positional play.

Lateral movement: Have the shooters move across the net, parallel to the goal crease, for shots on goal. With this action, the goaltenders have to learn to move across the net in timing with the attacker.

Pressure shooting: Contests between the shooter and goaltender are fun pressure situations. Penalty shot contests provide fun and skill development.

Two-on-none: Two attackers with no defenders give the goaltender excellent movement in defending the net.

Screen shots, tip-ins, deflected shots: These happen in a game, so they must be practiced. One method for this is to use the stationary shots drill with a player in from the goal to screen and tip-in the shots.

Throwing the puck: A coach or the other goaltender can throw the puck to precise locations so that the goaltender can work on special moves.

Following the puck behind the net: A player moves the puck back and forth behind the net, then tries to score. The goaltender must move accordingly.

These are only a few drills. The best drills are game-condition drills. Study of the goaltenders should reveal work areas that drills can be devised for.

Section 2:
Physical
Conditioning

Hockey is a demanding sport that requires a highly trained and fit body. There are no magic formulas to condition the body. Hard work and knowledge of the research are needed. Care must be taken not to overtrain the body. The conditioning process must not cross the line into a stressful situation. The body needs rest. Remember, exercise wears the body down, but rest rebuilds the body. Rest must meet the demands.

Chapter Four: Fitness and Conditioning

Getting the players into shape is not a difficult task. There are some guiding principles to help in devising a program. Conditioning is the process of developing energy potential through an exercise program.

Total fitness is the term used for an athlete's complete mental, social and physical fitness.

Physical fitness is the fitness of the physical body. This chapter is limited to the physical aspects of fitness. Mental factors like social aspects, depression, stress and personality are all factors that can affect the physical body.

HEALTH FITNESS

The following five fitness factors are important to the hockey player:

Cardio respiratory fitness is the fitness of the heart, lungs and blood. This fitness is what brings oxygen to the body for energy.

Muscular strength is the amount of force a muscle can accomplish in one contraction.

Muscular endurance is the ability of the muscle to exercise over time through many contractions.

Flexibility is the mobility of the joints and the stretch of the muscles.

Body fatness is the percentage of body fat.

SKILL FITNESS

The following are not health-fitness factors but skill-level factors. They are also important to the hockey player.

Agility is the ability to move efficiently and quickly in any direction.

Balance is maintaining control of the body in different positions.

Coordination is the ability of the agonist and the antagonist muscles to execute movement efficiently. Each muscle has a muscle that works against the other muscle. The triceps work against the biceps. When one contracts, the other must relax, or the movement will become inefficient.

CONDITIONING PRINCIPLES

The overload principle is the idea of increasing the demands to reach higher levels. In strength training, the weight is increased as the muscle gets stronger. In endurance training — like stops and starts — the numbers are increased as the player show more endurance.

The progression principle is increasing the demands of an exercise. Drills are designed for simplicity and then move into complexity. The skill progresses to the needed future demands by a series of progressions or steps.

The specificity principle is an exercise that must be specific to the desired outcome. Fast breaks are needed to play the game. Fast breaks are specific to the game, so fast breaks must be practiced similar to game conditions. Goaltenders must condition themselves with exercises that are specific to their needs and not just do the drills of the forwards. Practice and conditioning must be specific to the needs of the game.

PRACTICE FACTORS

Intensity can be practiced. Most practices should involve game-intensity demands. Some practices might be light, but care should be developed so that the players do not become careless or lackluster.

Frequency of the drills is based on the overload and progression principle. Is there adequate rest to meet the demands?

Duration is how long the drill or practice should be maintained.

DEVELOPING A PROGRAM

Goals should be set for the team and individuals. The goals must be realistic and in line with the player's abilities. Remember the progression principles. Start simple and work slowly into the more complex aspects.

Interest and motivation are important factors. Conditioning can be boring and painful, so the drills must be fun. The players must understand the need for top-level conditioning and be willing to pay the price. Early in the season, the motivation is high. Later into the season, motivation might become a problem, as every practice seems to be the same repetitions. Variety is helpful at this stage of the season. Remember the fun aspect of the practice sessions. All players — from youth to the pros — want to have enjoyable and fun practices but also learn to perform better.

The best drills for practice sessions are ones that emphasize game-condition situations. Study what the players are doing wrong in the games, then devise drills based on these situations.

Keep the practices moving. Eliminate dead time. Dead time has too many players standing around doing nothing. Keep everyone busy, and save the long lectures for the dressing room.

As the athletes fatigue during the practice session, do not let them fall into faulty thinking. Fatigue delays the thought process. Stress the mental aspects of the performance as well as the physical aspects.

Overtraining and staleness are serious problems and usually develop later in the season. The coach must continually look for signs of overtraining and boredom. Slowness of movement and thoughts, absentmindedness, lack of fun and humor and temper tantrums are some examples of this problems. Look for some things that are different. Overtraining is often a result of guilt feelings. The coach and players might feel the need for a break but feel too guilty to take a break. Sometimes, the work ethic becomes so overemphasized that the players become stale and bored.

Boredom and staleness are the result of lack of learning or lack of progression. The routine has become *too* routine. Nothing new is learned. The players feel there is no progression. The attitude becomes: "Why practice? We are not learning or progressing in our skills."

Rest is important to the athlete. Too much rest and the athlete will become lazy and logy. Adequate rest is essential. Exercise wears the body down. Rest rebuilds the body to the new demands. Lack of rest wears the body down so that the athlete might soon reach a state of chronic fatigue. A restless night's sleep before a game is not too serious if the athlete has been well-rested prior to the restless night. Many players do not sleep too well the night before a game, but they will still perform well during the game.

Good coaches are able to pace the conditioning process. They know when to ease up and when to make the extra demands. They often coordinate this with their game schedule, and they are able to alternate their hard workouts with the less demanding workouts to rest the body. It is best not to have two demanding workouts in a row. Alternate heavy and light workouts. Twenty-four hours is not always sufficient to recover from a demanding practice. Demanding days can have lots of conditioning drills, and light days can be used to work on skill development and strategy.

Athletes must train year-round. The off-season is a good time for strength development. If ice is not available year-round, the player can work on cardio respiratory and other fitness factors. Shooting can be practiced on a waxed board to a target or net. Kids play street hockey with rollerblades. There's no reason why adults can't do this. In fact, rollerblades are excellent means of skating when ice is unavailable. Soccer is an excellent game for off-ice conditioning.

Fatigue interferes with the thinking process. When a player makes mental errors on the ice, fatigue might be the cause. Fatigue slows the reflexes and the decision-making processes.

Always warm up before stretching the muscles. Do not stretch to warm up, as stretching the cold muscles can cause minute tears in the muscles, which, in time, will cause severe damage to the muscle and thus take the player out of action and into rehabilitation. Stretching should not be overdone. Stretch slow and easy. Some athletes do their stretching in the middle of the practice session or in the shower, when the body is nice and warm. To warm up the body, do several laps around the rink at slow speeds. As the body warms, then the speed can be increased, with even some half- to three-quarter-speed agility drills. Remember, it is a warmup, not a game-condition requirement.

Drink water as needed and even before it is needed. Water prevents dehydration. Drink it.

Heat can be a problem, as the player's uniform and equipment hold much of the heat to the body. Dry land workouts can be a problem if the temperature and humidity are high. High temperatures cause the body to sweat heavily, and the high humidity prevents the sweat from evaporating and cooling the body. The use of rubber or plastic suits to make the player sweat is a dangerous practice, as it can lead to dehydration, heat exhaustion and even heatstroke. Weight loss does occur with this method, but it is only dangerous water loss and not fat loss. If a player feels dizzy, nauseous and/or disoriented, then the player should be cooled immediately. Do not cool down too quickly and with too much cold as the body may go into shock. If it's serious, medical help might be needed.

AEROBIC ENDURANCE AND ANAEROBIC POWER

The body uses carbohydrates, fats and proteins as fuels for energy. Carbohydrates are the main source of energy, as they break down quickly. Fats are the secondary source for energy but are slow to break down for use. Proteins are used only when the supply of carbohydrates and fats is low. Proteins are mostly used for tissue repair. Food is broken down to form glucose or sugar. The glucose is stored in the muscles and blood for use as energy. The extra glucose is stored in the liver as glycogen. This glycogen is a reserve for when the blood and muscles run out of glucose. The breakdown of glucose for energy is a process called glycolysis. There is a fast glycolysis called anaerobic and a slow glycolysis called aerobic. The aerobic system means air (or containing oxygen), while the anaerobic system means no oxygen.

During quick fast breaks and movements, the body uses the anaerobic system of glucose/sugar in the blood and muscles. The glucose lasts for only about a minute at maximum effort. The energy comes directly from the glucose in the muscles and blood. No oxygen is used in the process. After this time frame, the body needs to rest to have the liver supply the muscles and blood with more glucose and oxygen. The aerobic system is used for less demanding effort. With slower activity, the body uses oxygen for the slow glycolysis to create energy.

Hockey uses both systems and often a little of each system at the same time. The body need oxygen for energy, so after the fast breaks, the player breathes heavily to build up the oxygen level. Good hockey players are able to pace themselves by applying both systems to the situation. Because of the demands, a hockey line shift is usually between one and two minutes. Any longer, if the demands are strong, will deplete the energy systems for immediate use. This is why it is a good idea to change lines before the energy systems run dry.

Under heavy demands on the anaerobic system, lactic acid is built up in the blood. Rest and heavy breathing are needed to replenish this system, as the oxygen intake helps to reprocess the lactic acid. In the aerobic system, lactic acid buildup is minimal because of the use of oxygen. Lactic acid is sometimes called the fatigue acid. As the body is conditioned and moves into peak condition, the body is able to better control the lactic acid buildup by clearing it from the system faster and more efficiently.

It is best to condition the player aerobically first. This means that in the early season, most of the conditioning is aerobic. As the aerobic system becomes more efficient, then the anaerobic system can enter the program. By doing the aerobic system first, the body adjusts to the new demands. The muscles are stretching and adjusting. Many coaches start the season with quick breaks and demanding stops and starts. Such tactics are very likely to cause many injuries and muscle problems. It is best to use the progression principle. Start with the fast breaks and stop and starts at half-speed. In a week or two, go to the three-quarter speed, and then, the next week, do full speed drills. Some coaches take the attitude "I'm going to show them who is running this team" or "They are going to see I mean business." These attitudes are detrimental and stupid.

INTERVAL TRAINING CONDITIONING

Interval training is a system utilized by track and field participants as well as swimmers. However, it is ideal for hockey because the game itself is an interval training system. The players are on the ice for a shift and then sit on the bench for two shifts.

Interval training is a specificity program. The conditioning program is specific to the needs of the player's position. Goaltenders will train differently than defensewomen, and, in turn, they will train differently than forwards. The basis of the program is the ratio between work and rest. If a 1-to-2 ratio is used, then the players work for one part and then rest for two parts. This means if the player is skating full speed for 15 seconds, then the player has 30 seconds to rest before she skates full speed again for 15 seconds. Repetitions are the number of times this drill is repeated.

When designing the interval program, the demands should start out easy, like a 1-to-3 or 1-to-4 ration. As proficiency increases, the ratios drop to 1-to-2 and 1-to-1. A 1-to-2 ratio is the most common for ice hockey, as this ratio meets the game-playing conditions. The players work/play for one part on the ice and then rest on the bench for two parts.

The rest phase must be sufficient to let the player's heart rate drop to about 140 beats per minute. Pushing the rest interval to short times does not help development. In fact, it hinders the conditioning process by activating too much stress to the body. Estimating the heart rate for the entire team is difficult. This might be done by having one player checking her pulse. With practice, a coach will be able to look at the player and estimate the ratio needed. The number of repetitions will also vary to the situation. Usually three repetitions completes a set. After each set, the players should have a good rest to get the heart rate down to 120 beats per minute before the next set starts.

When doing the interval training on the ice, the forwards are in one area, the defensewomen in another area and the goaltenders in their area. Each group will be doing drills for their specific skills, but all will be on the same ratios. An example would be to have the forwards along the board from the center ice area to the goal crease. The defensewomen are on the blue line, and the goaltenders are in front of each net. When the whistle blows, the forwards do stops and starts from the boards to the boards. The defensewomen do backward skating to the corner and pick up a puck and carry it back to the blue line. The goaltenders do one-knee slides from post to post. At the next whistle, all players stop to rest. These skills change to cover more skills that the players need. The advantage of this system is that individual skills are used for the conditioning process.

DRY LAND PROGRAMS

When ice is not available, then conditioning can be done outdoors. Fast breaks, hopping and running sideways, aerobic jogging, etc., are all helpful. Fast breaks should be performed with alternating starting legs so that the players learn to start quickly with either leg. Some players only use the same leg for all their quick breaks, failing to realize the delay to some starts.

Soccer is an excellent dry land game. It provides lots of running and other movements required in hockey. In most cases, it is best to break the team down into smaller sizes by having two or three games going at the same time. This way, each player gets more activity. Other games like basketball, field hockey, speedball, team handball and volleyball are also useful. Individual sports like badminton, bicycling, karate, racquetball, handball, swimming, table tennis and tennis are excellent not only for the conditioning but for the variety of activity. If ice is not available, we must not forget the rollerblade skates. These are great for the off-season, and you can actually play hockey when the ice is not available.

DEVELOPING MUSCULAR STRENGTH AND ENDURANCE

A weight-training program is beneficial to the players, but it can only develop muscular strength and muscular endurance. Cardio respiratory endurance is developed though aerobic training. Any weight-training program that develops the total body is sufficient. The agonist muscle and the antagonist muscle must be developed equally or the body becomes imbalanced and this can result in injuries. Do not overemphasis certain muscle groups.

The muscles do not know or care about the expense of the weight-training machines or barbells. The muscles are only concerned about the resistance against the muscles. Dumbbells or barbells work excellently. In fact, it has never been proven that the expensive machines do better than the free weights. Athletes should use barbells or dumbbells because when manipulating the weights, the athlete must maintain balance. When sitting in a machine, there is no balance factor to the movement. Controlling balance is vital to the athlete in any skill.

NUTRITION

Nutrition cannot replace proper conditioning. However, nutrition will help the body to be healthy and energetic. An entire book can cover this area. This is a hockey book and not a nutrition book. But here are some general guidelines: Eat a balanced diet. Eat a variety of foods. Have plenty of vegetables, fruits and grain products. Stay low in fats, although some fats are needed. Keep sugar, salt and sodium to a minimum.

The daily diet is more important than the pre-game meal. One meal before a game will not solve dietary problems. A high carbohydrate meal is often recommended, but some still prefer to have the steak and potatoes. Fatty foods and fried foods are not recommended for pre-game consumption. Sauces and condiments should be minimal.

Chapter Five: Injuries and Medical Problems

Injuries and medical problems should be considered from four aspects: prevention, diagnosis, treatment and rehabilitation.

PREVENTION

Conditioning/fitness, strength and flexibility are important factors in preventing an injury. Equipment is also important. Players need the proper equipment. Inexpensive equipment that results in an injury is not a money-saving factor. In fact, the money should go to what is underneath the jersey and not into the jersey. Diet may help prevent injuries, as a good diet means good energy and alertness to the athlete. Rest is also important to injury prevention. Players under stress — physically and mentally — become susceptible to injury. Good coaching and officiating also helps to control injuries. Minor problems should be checked out before they become major problems.

DIAGNOSIS

The coach or trainer can treat most minor injuries but must be aware that they are not medically trained doctors. When in doubt, find a doctor. When making the diagnosis, be aware that, sometimes, the pain is referred pain, as such pain is distant from the injury. Some injuries are latent in that they do not show until later in time. Head injuries are often latent injuries.

TREATMENT

The BASIC TREATMENT to an injury is: RICE

R = rest

I = ice (or cold)

C= compress (or wrap)

E = elevate

Cold reduces the swelling and might help in the pain. The ice (or cold) should be applied immediately to the injured area for 20 minutes every four hours. Heat should not be applied to the injured area until 24 to 48 hours after the injury. Frozen wet sponges make excellent ice packs, as they can help form to the area. The following are short and quick guidelines for injuries:

Abrasions

Treat as open wounds.

Athlete's Foot

There are many sprays, powders and creams to cure the fungus.

Blisters

A blister is caused by friction to the area. If the blister is filled with liquid, then the blister might best be drained by a sterilized needle. If needed, the blister can be covered with a felt pad with a hole cut out for the blister to fit into. This will help prevent further friction to the area so that healing can occur.

Charley Horse

This is a muscle spasm common to the upper thigh muscles. Basic treatment is needed. Be careful with this injury, as the muscle damage might be quite severe. Do not exercise the injury in the hopes that it will work its way out.

Contusion (Bruises)

Basic treatment. Protection might be need if the player

continues to play. No heat to the area.

Cramps

Can often be cured by stretching the muscle and with a short rest. Severe cramps might be caused by a diet deficiency, fatigue or a salt and vitamin deficiency.

Facial Injuries

These are bruises, cut and scrapes. Basic treatment is used. Look for the possibility of a more severe injury than what is shown. A black eye might mean severe eye damage. A bruise to the cheek might mean a cracked cheekbone.

Fractures

If a break is suspected, then the injury must be splinted immediately. Cold packs are immediately needed. When the injured player is put on a stretcher, slide it along the ice to the open door and then lift up. Medical attention is needed.

Head Injuries

All head injuries need immediate medical attention. The player should be taken out of the game, as most head injuries are latent and show problems later. Players who suffer head injuries should be under observation for the rest of the day and night.

Joint Injuries

Use basic treatment and get medical help. These can be serious.

Open Wound

This injury should be cleaned and disinfected. If needed, it can be covered with sterilized material, and ice packs can be applied. Stitches might be required and should be done within six hours.

Possible Neck and Spinal Injuries

Do not move! Ask the player if she can move. If she

cannot move, then assume spinal problems. If necessary, the players might have to go back to the dressing room until the injured player can be properly removed from the ice.

Rashes

Equipment can cause rashes to the skin. The main problem is if the rash becomes infected.

Sprains

This is a tearing or overstretching of a ligament. Basic treatment is immediately needed. Sprains can range from light to severe. If the sprain shows severity, then medical attention might be needed.

Strains

A strain is an overstretching of the muscle. Basic treatment.

Teeth Injuries

This is for the dentist.

Wind Knocked Out

Loosening equipment might help. The victim will usually return to normal in a short time. Check for further abdominal injuries.

Rehabilitation

Rehabilitation is necessary to get the athlete back into action as quickly as possible. Also, it is necessary to return the athlete back to her health for a normal lifestyle. Medical help is often necessary.

Some Basic Guidelines

Remain calm: Present the image of being in control. By remaining calm, you will be better able to control the situation as well as make correct decisions.

Never assume the role of a physician: Put the responsibility of the diagnosis on a trained physician. A coach is not trained in medical diagnosis.

Never do anything that could be interpreted as negligence: As a coach, you have assumed responsibility for your players. Look after them.

Never move a player with a suspected serious injury: Leave the movement to qualified people.

Do not take chances with the hope that nothing might happen: Do not leave the players unsupervised, as this is when something might happen.

Do not put a player or team into an unsafe or dangerous situation: Safety is a must.

Never play a player after an injury that might be a serious injury: Some injuries, especially head injuries, are latent. Take no chances.

Section 3:
Mental Skills

Athletes are becoming more agreeable to the practice of mental skills. The mental skills do work, but they require practice just like the physical skills. This section deals with mental skills as well as the practice of neuro-linguistic programming (NLP) and zen.

Chapter Six:
Mental Skills

Mental skills are easy to understand and learn. The effectiveness of mental skills is based on how they perform under pressure or stressful situations. It is easy to ignore distractions during practice, but can the player ignore the distractions under game conditions? When every shot on goal is important, when every backcheck is important, when the score is important, when all such things are important, the mind must be in control.

Thought-stopping is an excellent technique to bring the mind back in control. When the mind is distracted, the player simply stops the present-thought process and reorganizes her thoughts and starts all over again. This is often easy in a no-distraction or pressureless situation. The real talent is to be able to execute the skill in pressure situations. This takes practice.

MOTIVATION

Coaches are assessed by their ability to motivate their players. This is not really an accurate assessment of the coach's ability. Motivation is the player's responsibility as well as the coach's. "You can lead a horse to water, but you can't make her drink." This statement seems to sum up the coach. The coach can lead and help the players, but in the final analysis, the players must have the desire and motivation to perform. Good coaches do not necessarily motivate their players, but they can de-motivate a player or team by poor planning, poor judgments and poor decisions. Players are motivated. They do not have to be motivated. If they were not motivated, they would not be playing. Good coaching maintains the motivation. Poor coaching weakens or kills the motivation. Athletes must take responsibility for their motivation. Coaches can help, but they are not solely responsible for an athlete's motivation. If a player lacks motivation, then the coach must take steps to rectify the situation, with even the possibility of dismissing the player from the team.

PSYCHOLOGICAL STRATEGIES

Mental strategies are helpful, but they cannot replace lack of skill. Physical skills must be developed to their maximum so that they can be further enhanced by mental skills. Psychology will not make up for a lack of skill. Many athletes have the physical skill during practice or pressureless situations but are under-performing in game conditions. Fear of injury or pain (like going into the corners) can hinder performance. Stress and anxiety might be problems. Social problems might even cause poor playing. Psychological skills can help in these situations. The mental skills are needed to let the player perform to her maximum and bring out her true potential.

Potential is an interesting subject to the coach. Potential means a player has the ability to perform better. Sometimes, it just takes time and experience. One thing is for sure: You do not win games on potential. The player must perform to her ability at the present time. Mental strategies can help bring out this potential.

MENTAL STRATEGIES WHEN NOT PERFORMING

To work on mind control, the athlete should follow this sequence: goal setting, assessment, relaxation, imagery, evaluation.

Goal setting: This is the first step to mental control. What do you want? What areas do you need to work on? Where do you need improvement? These types of questions must be answered. Make your goals realistic and set in a progressive manner. Start with simple goals and then progress to building on each goal until you reach your long-term goal.

Assessment: Assess what skills need development. Is it puck control, pass receiving, fear of the corners, etc.? Once the assessment is completed, then work on one skill at a time. Do not try to accomplish too much too quickly. Too much (overload) will only hamper results.

Relaxation: Learn to relax the body. Sit or lie comfortably. Feel your body relax. Start at the feet and focus on relaxing them. As you feel the feet relax and go limp, move on to relaxing the legs. Progress your way up the body until the body is completely relaxed. When you are completely relaxed, then move on to the next phase.

Imagery: This is where you run movies in your mind. For example, see yourself accomplishing the goals you set. See yourself making the puck-control moves you desire. See yourself showing no fear going into the corner for the puck. Let this movie play in your mind. Do this daily, and in time, the movie will become a part of you, and you will act accordingly to the movie. In time, you will believe the movie. When you believe, your confidence soars.

Evaluation: In time, you assess your improvement. Do you need more time with the mental skill you are now using or is it time to move on to another skill? The evaluation process is ongoing. Evaluation is a form of feedback. Learning requires feedback. No feedback — no learning.

MENTAL STRATEGIES WHEN PERFORMING

The following strategies might seem simple, and you might feel that you already do them. They are simple, but are you able to use them effectively in pressure situations? Performance under pressure is the ultimate goal.

Thought-stopping: This is highly effective and simple. When the mind is not focused on the task at hand or is distracted, the athlete simply stops the thought process and refocuses the mind in a new direction. Distractions often cause the mind to wander in the wrong direction. Thought-stopping can reorganize it. This skill takes practice because under pressure, the distractions are powerful.

Self-talk: This skill is where the athlete talks to herself. She tells herself what to do. Sometimes, this talk is done with imagery of picturing the talk. Keep the self-talk positive to develop positive pictures. Negative self-talk creates negative pictures.

Rational thinking: This is realistic thinking. Do not use self-talk or positive thinking to take you beyond your capabilities or skills. Rational thinking will turn your mistakes into learning situations. Mistakes will happen. You must learn to cope with them.

False assumptions: False assumptions are a result of poor realistic thinking and not using rational thinking. Some athletes mess up when assuming they can do things they really can't do. The athlete must make an honest evaluation of her skill and ability. If they are weak in an area, they must improve the area and not assume there is no problem.

Positive thinking: No matter how positive one is, there is no value if they do not have the skill to back up the thought process. "You must walk the talk." Successful results from positive thinking are a result of the skill level being able to achieve the results. Positive thinking needs rational thinking.

Perceptions: Things are how we perceive them. How we perceive a situation will make us calm or stressful. If we perceive that going into the corner for the puck is dangerous and painful, then we created a stressful situation. If we perceive that going into the corners is fun and desirable, then there is no stress created. Penalty killing is perceived as fun and important, although some do not like it. Every player might not have the same perception to every situation. To cope with unpleasant situations, learn to perceive the situation differently.

Very often, one's perception of the situation is based on past experiences. Past successful situations will be perceived as present successful situations. Past disasters will also be perceived as present disasters. The player must focus on the past successful experiences to cope with the present. To erase the past disasters, the athlete can use the strategy in the "Mental Strategies When Not Performing" section previous to this one. Another way to cope with past disasters is to work with the coach during practice sessions on these disaster situations to build up experience and confidence. As the situation improves, the negative perceptions will fade away and be replaced by successful perceptions.

Confidence: Confidence is the result of a thorough knowledge of one's ability. Confidence in not necessarily a result of positive thinking. Confidence is not a result of arrogance or bragging. Confidence develops from past successful experiences. The athlete knows her capabilities — what will or won't work. False confidence is like false assumptions.

MEDITATION

Some athletes meditate and have excellent results. Some athletes have found no value in it. The main purpose of meditation is to relax the body and mind. Anxiety, frustration and other mental factors have been controlled by meditation. Good performance is the result of a clear mind. Confused thoughts cloud the mind and, in turn, hamper performance. Meditation might clear your mind for you.

AUTOGENIC TRAINING

This is like meditation and imagery to relax the body. The body is relaxed, with the mind focusing on the various body parts becoming heavy and warm. When the body is relaxed, then imagery of various skills (the movie) runs through the mind. It is very similar to the strategy outline previously in "Mental Strategies When Not Performing."

CHOKING

All mistakes and poor performances are not choking. Sometimes, it is just the percentages falling into place. Every shot is not a goal scored. When the goal is highly needed and the shot does not go in the net, it cannot always be assumed it was a choke. These things happen. Sometimes, the choke might be the result of poor coaching in that the coach failed to practice for this situation.

A true choke is when the athlete's mind goes blank or confused and she focuses on the wrong things. When choking occurs, good coaches develop drills and practice situations to correct such problems and to help cope with these problems in the future.

Chapter Seven:
Zen and Hockey

Zen is simplicity. To learn Zen, you must practice Zen. To learn concentration, you must practice concentration. In time, the concentration becomes automatic and a part of you. You concentrate unconsciously. No tension. No forcing. It happens. Skill-learning is the same. To learn a skill, you practice the skill. In time, the skill becomes automatic and a part of you. You perform the skill automatically and unconsciously. No tension. No forcing. It happens.

HERE AND NOW — THE PRESENT

Playing hockey is in the here and now state. The present is important. Not the past or future. Performance is dependent on the present moment, not what you did in the past or what will happen in the future. The mind must be focused on the present. Forget the outcome or future, as the desired future will not happen unless the present is taken care of correctly.

AWARENESS

Hockey is a game of awareness. The players must be completely aware of what is going on. What is the flow of the game? Are they aware of what they are doing in relationship to their teammates and opposition? It is a oneness. The player and the surroundings are one. The player is the game. The player is the puck. The puck is the player. It is all one.

Awareness is an experience. It must be experienced. It must be practiced. Awareness helps in team play with passing and positional play. The aware player moves with the flow of the game. It is unconscious. It is automatic.

Hockey players learn mastery of the self. A mastery that carries over into other life situations. A mastery of awareness with the rink, opposition and teammates. A state of supreme flow with everything in harmony. This state is not always achieved, but when it happens, the results are phenomenal. This state cannot be forced. It just happens. Practice for this state makes it happen.

The mind creates the state of flow. A confused mind prevents things from happening. A doubting mind creates hesitation in performance. When the mind is dysfunctional, the body is dysfunctional. The mind must be clear and alert. The mind must be focused on the present.

CONCENTRATION

Concentration cannot be forced. It happens. Take a ball or an object and toss it in the air, then catch it. Notice how easy that was. There was no strain or tension. You tossed the ball and caught it. There were no distracting thoughts of how to execute the skill, no thoughts of who was watching, no thoughts of failure, etc. There were no thoughts. Just a focus on the ball going up and down and into the hand. This is concentration.

Some athletes try so hard to concentrate that they are concentrating on how to concentrate. They go into tension. They try so hard that they fail. You cannot force concentration. You just have to focus on the task and forget about the outcome and other distractions. Let it happen. Thinking of the outcome hampers performance in the present. Concentration is for the moment only. Relax the body and mind. Let it happen.

HIGH SPIRIT AND LOW SPIRIT

When performing, a player must not let herself achieve too high a spirit or too low a spirit. Both emotions are detrimental to performance. Some teams and players are of such a high spirit in the dying minutes of an important winning game that their play becomes ragged and uncertain. They are celebrating before the game is over.

High and low spirits alter the mind's thought process and take the athlete out of the present. Good performers are cool and collected. Bad breaks happen, but they move on and continue with the same cool, calm, collected, clear and alert mind. The bad breaks are in the past. Learn from them, but do not let them interfere with the present.

NEVER SHOW DEFEAT OR WEAKNESS

This is important. Showing defeat or weakness lets the opposition read your mind and performance. When a team hangs their head in defeat before the game is over, the opposition rallies in confidence. Pressure is off the opposition. The opposition now becomes dangerous and efficient.

By not showing defeat or weakness, the opposition must always be on guard. The opposition cannot be relaxed or confident. Not showing defeat and remaining confident can change the momentum of the game. Phenomenal results have been achieved by not giving up. When you give up, there is no chance of success. Comebacks are not achieved by negative thinking.

ACT AS IF

By "acting as if" you are winning or playing well, there is a good chance that you will play well. "Acting as if" helps to develop confidence. Also, it can put you in the present. Showing defeat or weakness means you are focusing on the outcome or past, not the present. If you "act as if" long enough, you will come to believe. When you believe, you might just become successful.

FEAR

Fear is the first enemy. Past experiences and thoughts of the future create fear. It is these perceptions that create the fear. In hockey — in fact, in all athletics — fear is a constant companion. Fear is a battle with the self. It is a battle with how the situation is perceived. All athletes know and experience fear. The good ones know how to control it.

Fear is like a shadow: It has no substance. Fear is often created by the uncertainty of the situation. Fear is a threat to the ego in that the player might look bad or fail in her performance. Fear prevents a player from letting go. Let go of the ego so that it cannot be under attack. Free the mind and take control. Become the situation. Be the situation.

TENSION

Mental and physical tension deteriorates skill execution. A player must recognize when tension is creeping into her performance. Extreme tension is easily recognized, but the subtle tension is difficult. When not playing, the player should tense various muscles and relax them. In time, the difference between a relaxed muscle and a tense muscle will be readily noticeable. The next stage is to tense the muscle lightly and then relax. In time, one can readily notice the difference between a slightly tense muscle and a relaxed muscle.

It is essential for the hockey player to relax while sitting on the bench for her next shift. A tense body while on the bench is wasting valuable energy. When on the bench after a shift, the player should relax the various parts of the body for the next shift.

PATIENCE

Good players know patience. They do not panic or worry. They do not push the clock. Panic and worry are playing to the future, not the moment.

HONOR YOUR OPPONENT

Athletes should honor their opponent. Your opponent is not the enemy. Your opponent is there to help you perform well, to test you, to make you excel and to give you the opportunity to show your best. The better the opponent, the better the challenge. Without an opponent, you have no opportunity to show your skills. The real enemy is yourself. How you control the self. How you perform. Do not let your opponent control you. If you let your opponent control you, then you have failed. "You control you."

THE SELF

The opposition is not your opponent. Your opponent is yourself. You are the one that you have to control. You cannot control the opposition if you cannot control yourself. Tom Watson was going into the last round of a major PGA tournament with a one-stroke lead. During an interview, he was asked about all the great players that were within one or two strokes of him and which competitors he feared the most. His reply was that the one he feared the most was himself.

ENLIGHTENMENT

The mind controls the game. The use of the mind determines the outcome. Better warriors think better. Better warriors have better mind control. The best warrior has the best mind control of all the warriors. Hockey players are warriors.

Mind control is the key to hockey enlightenment. The great Japanese swordsman Munenori claimed in his *Book of Five Rings* that he used swordsmanship to learn how to control his mind. As his mind developed, his swordsmanship was able to perform through his will. It is the same for hockey players. Use hockey to learn how to control the mind, then let hockey be performed by the will.

The mind controls the body. When we use our will, we are using our intuition. The mind is the mind. The brain is the physical organ, not the mind. The mind is in the muscles, bones, skin, etc. The mind is in the whole body. With the mind in the body, the body is able to react quickly and without thought. Thinking takes time. The mind is always ready if it is alert and aware. Enlightenment is when the player lets the mind move into the body.

To reach enlightenment, the player must master all things. If you have not mastered a skill, you will have doubts about being able to perform that skill. Your mind has doubts, then your body has doubts. Master your skills so that no doubts persist.

OBSESSION

It is a disease to be obsessed with the thought of winning.
It is a disease to be obsessed with the thought of failure.
It is a disease to be obsessed with the thought of anything.

Obsession sickens and clouds the mind. The obsessed mind gives an incomplete picture. The obsessed mind has become attached. A warrior's mind must never become attached to one thing. It must be open and clear. The attached mind is a stuck mind, a slow mind, a diseased mind. The enlightened athlete does not let her mind become obsessed.

When enlightened, the player sees with the mind. The eyes then see it. The body then performs automatically in the intuition stage. The awareness of the situation through the mind and eyes lets the athlete perform intuitively.

Chapter Eight: Neuro-Linguistic Programming (NLP)

Neuro-linguistic programming (NLP) is a new psychology that is used for learning various types of skills. The basis of NLP is on modeling the skills of successful people who are able to execute the desired skill. The successful person is analyzed, and then you model these characteristics. It is a form of imitation.

Youngsters learn skills this way. They watch a hockey player and then they imitate her moves and mannerisms. The kid looks at the skill, pictures it in her mind and then executes the skill. If the trial is unsuccessful, then the attempt is repeated as often as necessary to acquire the skill. Kids do not overanalyze. They see it. They do it.

Adults overanalyze learning. The become bogged down in detail. Their minds are confused and clouded with too much thinking. Adults would be better to learn like a kid. Free the mind. Do it.

To learn a skill, you must know exactly what you want to achieve. Develop a clear picture in your mind of the skill. Make a movie in the mind. Play the movie often so that it continues to be more familiar to you. Play the movie while you practice. In time, the movies will make the moves for you. It will become automatic. Your body will respond to the movie.

Once you learn the skill, you forget it. Your trust is needed to let it happen when you need the skill. Your unconscious will execute the skill. The skill becomes a "stop learning process" and becomes a "doing process." When the skill is needed, just focus on your objective.

Forget everything else. No distractions. Just let the skill happen.

As you see the situation develop, your eyesight will trigger the skill needed. Your body will respond automatically to what you see by calling up the required skill. The player must let this happen. If the player responds with further input, the skill will suffer.

We often hear the expression of "the empty mind." The empty mind is the clear mind that is not cluttered with distractions. Distractions interfere with performance. The empty mind lets the body perform the skill with no interference. The conscious mind operates too slowly for most skills. The unconscious mind is fast — more than fast enough for skill execution. The unconscious mind is like a reflex: It executes with no thought patterns to delay the process.

NLP is designed to control your mind and emotions. Emotions play a critical role in performance. Emotions affect your thinking and skill execution for the good or the bad. Good emotions can help your confidence. Bad emotions can destroy your confidence. The mind must control the body and emotions. Emotional control can be learned with NLP in the same way a physical skill is learned (see Chapter Six on mental skills).

ANCHORS OR TRIGGERS

An anchor, or trigger, is something that triggers a certain response. The sight of a snake often triggers fear. A puck in the corner of the rink with an opponent charging after it might trigger fear in some players. There are many situations that trigger fear in some players. Unfortunately, most triggers are negative. If a situation can trigger a negative response, then why can't a situation trigger a positive response? Changing one's perception of the situation can help.

Coaches can develop drills for situations that are perceived as negative by some players. Let's use the fear of corners as an example. The drill sets up the situation where the player goes into the corner with an opponent for the puck. This situation immediately sets up the fear perception. Continued work on this drill brings about familiarity to the situation. In time, the player gains confidence as she experiences more successful chances in coping with the skill. Off the ice, she practices her imagery skill for this the situation. In time, her perception begins to change from a negative to a positive. She is now cured.

Triggers can be developed for almost any situation. When carrying the puck for a one-on-one situation, the puck carrier looks for the crossing-over action of the defender's leg. The crossing over leg is the trigger for the puck carrier to move the other way. A shooter can fake the goaltender and wait for the move of the goaltender (the trigger) as to when and where to make the shot.

When off the ice, the use of imagery can help to develop triggers. The athlete puts herself in a state of relaxation. When relaxed, she then develops a movie of the skill she wants. She then develops a movie of the skill and looks for a trigger that will be used to set up the skill. If she is working on the fear of corners, the trigger is when the puck is in the corner. In the movie, she sees the puck in the corner and her body reacts automatically. There is no thought or analysis. The movie is triggered and the body responds. With practice, this skill will become indelible on the mind. When this happens, the player will execute with no fear when under game conditions. This example will work for other skills, like making the goaltender make the first move and then taking the shot.

Sometimes, it is good to reinforce these triggers even after you have become successful with the desired skill. Sometimes, you might have to develop a sequence of triggers for some situations. For example, if you have a trigger for the opposition's defensewoman crossing the leg and the defensewoman does not cross her leg, then you might have to make another fake and look for another trigger.

Learning a breakout play is another example of a sequence of triggers. When the defensewoman makes a pass to the right wing (the trigger), visualize your move. If the pass goes to the centerwoman (the trigger), visualize your move. The player makes movies in her mind of the sequence of events and her response to each pass. Practice this until it is indelible in the mind. She is now able to respond on the ice correctly. A habit is formed.

CHEVREUL'S PENDULUM

Take a string about 12 inches long. Attach a paper clip to the end. With your elbow resting on the tabletop, hold the string with the thumb and fingers and let the string hang down with the paper clip at the bottom of the string. Do not move the hand or fingers. Focus on the paper clip and visualize the clip moving back and forth. In a short time, the clip will move back and forth. Now change the visualization to the clip moving from side to side. Soon, it will do this. Change the focus to the clip moving in a circle, and soon, it will do this. Notice how the clip moves to the mind as you hold the hand still and steady.

To some, this might be strange or mysterious. Actually, it is not. Your fingers are actually moving the paper clip through your subconscious. The mind controls the body — and even the subconscious. This experiment shows how we simply have to let the mind take control. Let it happen. Let the mind work with no distraction. A clear mind. An empty mind.

EXCUSES

Excuses build negative pictures. Excuses are just facts that you have to believe in order to "save face." You have to justify your statements. You cannot be wrong. The excuse is a reason — a weak reason — for your failure. It is an attempt to save embarrassment.

If a player feels her excuse is legitimate, then she should talk to the coach after practice or the game. Sometimes, the excuse might be valid and the coach might want to change strategy or philosophy.

WORRY

Worry is a form of negative rehearsal or negative imagery. Worry pictures bad thing or thoughts. Worry is about thinking in the future, not the present. Negative pictures from worry can create indelible pictures in the mind, which in turn cause poor performance by the body.

SEE IT, FEEL IT, DO IT

"See it, feel it, do it" is a simple formula using NLP to perform a skill. The formula says it all.

DAYDREAMING

Daydreaming is a form of imagery/visualization. People daydream. Daydreaming shuts out all distractions. The daydreamer is focused on the dream only. Kids daydream of becoming hockey stars. They daydream of successful plays and skill execution. They role-play their favorite heroes and stars and imitate them. They are modeling the star hockey players. As mentioned earlier, modeling and imitating are the basis for NLP.

Adults should follow the kids in this technique. Many successful people have daydreamed their way to success. We often hear an athlete say "I dreamed of this day" or "It's a dream come true." Actors, musicians, business people, athletes, etc., have all made these statements.

Daydreaming seems to have a negative connotation. This is unfortunate, as daydreaming is just another form of NLP. It can be beneficial.

FAKE IT UNTIL YOU MAKE IT

This is another form of the "act as if" philosophy. You control your emotions. You can be happy or sad. It is your choice. If you want to be confident, then fake it and act confident. Play the role. NLP is role-playing. In time, it will become automatic. It will become a habit. The habit becomes part of your subconscious. It will be there when needed.

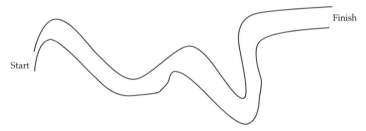

A visualization or imagery test.

Draw two parallel lines something like in the above diagram. Have the player look at the diagram and place a pen at the start. The player then closes her eyes and tries to trace the pencil from start to finish without touching or crossing the line. Players with good imagery skills will do fairly well. Poor imagery skill will readily show.

Section 4:
Coaching Duties

Coaches have many duties other than teaching skills. These duties are important, as the success of a team often depends on such duties. The coach can set the mood for the team.

Chapter Nine: Practice Planning

MURPHY'S LAW

Always plan for Murphy's Law: "Whatever can go wrong will go wrong." Sometimes, the unexpected happens. Are you prepared to continue with practice despite the problems?

PRESEASON

This is the time to prepare for the season. Determine your goals and philosophy. Make sure these goals are clear to the players as well as yourself. Plan how you will progress through the season to bring about your style of play. Start the season organized. Changes can still be made as needed or as situations change. Plan so that you know where you are going and how you are going to get there.

DRESSING ROOM TALKS

Have your dressing room organized (if you have one). A small, portable marker board for chalk talks will be needed if the dressing room does not have one. Do your long talks in the dressing room, not on the ice. In fact, it is a good idea to explain things like new drills in the dressing room so that less explanation is used on the ice.

DEMONSTRATIONS

When demonstrating on the ice, make sure the demo is accurate. A sloppy demo or an incorrect demo gives the players a poor picture to rely on. Use a player to demonstrate while the coach gives commentary on the moves. The coach can easily see if the demo is not perfected by the player and can easily correct it. If the coach is demonstrating, there is no way to tell if it is perfect. With age, some coaches often lose some of their skills.

When a coach demonstrates shooting, it is best not to release the puck. If the coach releases the puck, then the focus of attention by the players is on the puck and not on the mechanics of the shot. When this happens, the players are focusing on the results of the skill rather than the techniques of the skill.

To get the players to focus on the mechanics, it is sometimes a good idea to demonstrate the skill in slow motion. From the demo, have the player perform the skill in slow motion to get the feel. With practice, slowly move into faster and faster movements.

Coaches must never use a demonstration to "show off." Some old has-beens like to demonstrate everything. This is not teaching.

Every demonstration must be followed with the key points or moves. What are the key moves that will accomplish the skill? A key move is a move that will often trigger several other moves correctly.

DRILLS

The best drills are taken from game situations. During games, the coach should make a note of things that have to be practiced next practice. Coaches should keep a small notebook with them so that there is a record of what to work on. This way, there is less of a chance of forgetting something.

Drills are a supplement to the team's strategy or style of play. Passing drills, shooting drills, etc., should be executed exactly as in game situations. Drills should be designed to accomplish more than one skill. A drill that just works on passes might be time-consuming, as only one skill is practiced. Drills that involve skating, puck control, passing and shooting to a game strategy are most effective. As the season progresses, it is best to add variety to the drills. This can help prevent boredom from the same old routine.

It is best to add pressure to the drills. Pressure brings the drills closer to game conditions.

Never assume that because you did a drill, it will automatically be functional under game conditions. Failure to execute under game conditions is often the result of pressure. Sometimes, it is a failure to recognize the situation. In either case, it is back to more practice. The practice drill might have to be adjusted, but do not give up. If the drill is a good one, the players will catch on and perform under game conditions. Youngsters are vulnerable to this problem. They get so good at the drill that they fail to see it as a game situation. In time, they will catch on. Situations like these require patience by the coach. These drills should be coordinated with game-condition scrimmage. Do the drills and then scrimmage.

PRACTICE PLANNING

The following is a sample practice plan.

WEEKLY TIME SCHEDULE

Monday	90 minutes
Tuesday	90 minutes
Wednesday	0 minutes
Thursday	60 minutes
Friday	60 minutes
Saturday	Game
Sunday	0 minutes
Total	300 minutes

WEEKLY BREAKDOWN

Skating and conditioning	60 minutes
Puck control	30 minutes
Offense	30 minutes
Defense	30 minutes
Game situations	120 minutes
<u>Miscellaneous</u>	<u>30 minutes</u>
Total	300 minutes

DAILY PLAN FOR MONDAY: 90 MINUTES

Warmup laps	2 minutes
Figure Eights	2 minutes
Double give and go	3 minutes
etc.	

MASTER PRACTICE SHEET

This sheet keeps a record of how much time was spent on each skill. If mistakes are occurring, then a check of the record sheet might give the reason. The reason might be a lack of practice time. If sufficient practice time is provided, then maybe the drill or learning situation must be revised. The numbers represent minutes.

NOVEMBER	*1*	*2*	*3 . . . .*
Conditioning	10	20	10
Skating	10	10	10
Stickhandling		5	
Passing	10	10	10
Shooting		10	
Checking			
Goaltending	10	5	5
Defensewomen		10	

Forwards		10	10
Offensive play		20	
Defensive play	10		10
Face-offs	10		
Penalty killing	20		
Power play	20		
Pulled goalie			
Line changes			
Broken stick			
Injuries			
Scrimmage	30		
Totals	130	100	55

EQUIPMENT
Do not cut corners in this area. It is as simple as that.

MANAGERS
The selection of a manager is extremely important. Good managers help with team morale. The manager is often the link between the players and coach. A manager can provide valuable information about the players. If the team has more than one manager, then each manager must be assigned specific duties so that there is no conflict in duties and nothing fails to get done.

TEAM CAPTAINS
Captains can be appointed or elected. The choice is up to the coach. The coach assigns the captain's responsibilities. Some captains have specific responsibilities; some simply are given the honor. The coach must decide on the way to go.

HANDLING PLAYERS
The players are not robots. They are human beings. They have feelings, they have fears and attitudes, and

they have personalities. Coaches must understand the players. Knowledge of the players will help in coaching them.

As players move up in age and league status, the competition becomes keener and tougher. The better players remain, and the poorer players leave. First-year players who moved up to a higher status might have difficulty adjusting physically as well as socially. Some can cope with the playing skill level but have difficulty with the social aspect. Some players were stars at the lower level and are now just another player at the higher level. These are examples of stressful situations to the player. Coaches must deal with these problems and bring the players along to their full potential. Mishandling such players might destroy future stars.

SELECTING THE TEAM

This is a difficult task. Every player must be given a fair chance. If a player is cut, and she feels it was a poor decision, then it might be a good idea to give her another chance. Such a practice shows a sense of fairness to the players. Sometimes, a player is not ready for tryouts at the beginning of the season. The reasons vary from sickness to family problems. Good coaches are not too quick to make cuts.

NAME	NO.	SKATING	SHOOTING	PASSING	PASS RECEIVING	STICK HANDLING	HOCKEY SENSE	POTENTIAL	RATING	COMMENTS
Walls	2	1	2	2	3	3	2	1	14	Good Prospect
Jones	8	5	2	4	5	4	5	4	29	No chance
Dunn	4	2	3	3	3	2	2	1	16	Promise

Figure 9-1: A Rating System for Team Selection

Some coaches have used people in the stands to rate the players during practices (figure 9-1). Some coaches decide themselves or with their assistants. Some coaches use skill tests to help with the evaluation process.

SKILL TESTS

Skill tests are an interesting aspect to coaching. They are helpful to team selection and team competitiveness. The players love the action.They also see how they rank with the other players.

Puck Carry Test

The puck is placed on the blue line and the player weaves around each obstacle.

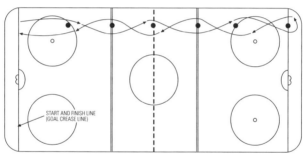

Figure 9-2: Puck Carry Test

Speed Forward and Speed Backward Test

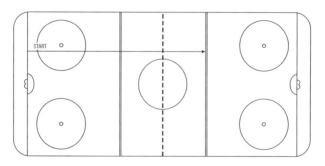

Figure 9-3: Speed Forward and Backward Test

Agility Test

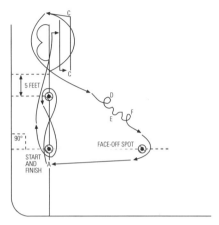

Figure 9-4: Agility Test

Shooting Test

A target can be set up in the goal. An object can be hung from the top crossbar.

Passing Test

A hockey stick is placed on the ice between the red line and the blue line. The player must skate full speed over the blue line and pass to the red line mark on the boards before hitting the hockey stick. If the red line is too small, then use a larger target. A wooden two-by-four of desired size can be painted red, laid on the ice at the red line and used as a target (figure 9-5).

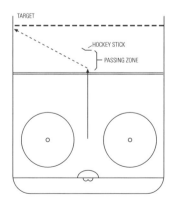

Figure 9-5: Passing Test

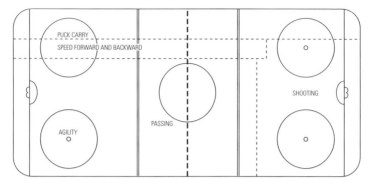

Figure 9-6: Skill Testing Stations

Testing layout

A coach can administer each test him or herself or set up stations as in figure 9-6. The use of stations can speed up the testing.

THE PREGAME WARMUP

The pregame warmup should include as many skills as possible. A sample warmup follows:

1. Each player carries a puck onto the ice and stickhandles around her half of the rink with the team in single file. On the captain's command, they change directions.

2. The players join with partners and repeat the above drill but pass back and forth to each other.

3. On command, the players position themselves for two-on-one drills, alternating from each side of the rink. After each rush, the players go to the other side.

4. On command, the players line up in their line formations. A defensewoman passes the puck out from the corner to the centerwoman for a line rush to the goal with many passes.

5. On command, a few more laps around their end and into the dressing room.

BETWEEN PERIODS OF A GAME

This is a critical time period. It should be used for rest and reorganization. It is best to let the players settle down before talking or even yelling at them. Tempers might be high during the first minute of the break, so let them calm down.

AFTER THE GAME

When the game is over, there is nothing that will change the outcome. Severe criticism might best be left until the next practice. By waiting, the players have time to settle down and reevaluate the game. The same applies to the coach. This waiting period sometimes gives a different perspective of the game. Game evaluations are critical to future performance, and sometimes, a little extra thought time is needed. Hard feelings and anger can easily be created by rash criticism immediately after a game. Cool heads must prevail.

Chapter Ten: Statistics, Coaching Aids and Scouting

All messages from the coach must be clear and easily understood. The following might be helpful to the coach and players.

CALENDAR OF EVENTS

This should be posted at a convenient place for all to see. Usually, it is best near the exit door so that the players can check it while leaving. This calendar gives the players a quick look at what is ahead with time requirements. The calendar should be large enough so that the printing can be easily read from a distance.

Sunday	Monday	Tuesday	Wednesday	Thursday	Friday	Saturday
28	PRACTICE 3:00 P.M. (SWEATSUIT ONLY) 29	PRACTICE 4:00 P.M. 30	MEETING 2:30 PRACTICE 3:30 P.M. 1	PRACTICE 3:00 P.M. 2	PRACTICE 2:00 P.M. 3	PRACTICE 9:00 P.M. 4
5	PRACTICE 3:00 P.M. (FULL GEAR) 6	PRACTICE 4:00 P.M. 7	PRACTICE 3:30 P.M. 8	PRACTICE 12:00 NOON 2:30 PACK 9	GAME AT 8:00 P.M. 10	GAME AT 8:00 P.M. 11
12	PRACTICE 3:00 P.M. (SWEATSUIT) 13	PRACTICE 4:00 P.M. 14	HOME			

Figure 10-1: Calendar of Events

CHALK OR MARKING BOARD AND MAGNETIC BOARDS

The dressing room should have a chalk or marking board for diagramming plays and drills. If there is not one in the dressing room, then portable ones are available from various companies. The magnetic boards are easy to use, as magnets represent the players and are easily moved around to various positions.

VIDEO

Video replays are almost standard equipment with most coaches. They are helpful, if used properly. Sometimes, it is difficult to get a good overall view of team play, as some rinks do not have the height requirements for the camera.

A NOTEPAD

A coach should carry this around in a pocket or purse, as good ideas strike any time. Write the idea down before it is forgotten. The small notepad should also be used during games and practices. During a game, important ideas are written down for use between periods, after the game or next practice. Do not always rely on memory.

A SMALL TAPE RECORDER

Some use these for scouting teams. Some find the notepad better and less of a problem to carry.

MUSIC

Some coaches use music during the warmup drills. It might help with the rhythm of the skating drills. Many players like music for the warmup and for the dressing rooms. Some feel it eases the pressure and relaxes them. A coach might have to experiment with the use and type of music.

SHOT CHARTS

Many companies now have standard shot charts. These are quite good. If desired, a coach can make his or her own.

GOALS SCORED CHART

This chart shows where the goals were scored (figure 10-2). Some shot charts have these. As the season

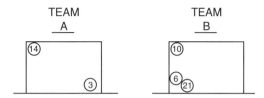

Figure 10-2: Goals Scored Chart

progresses, these charts will show if there is a trend as to where in the net the puck goes. These trends might show a weakness in goaltending or protection of the net by defensewomen and/or forwards.

FACE-OFF CHARTS

A record of face-offs will also show weaknesses and strengths of certain individuals. This can be valuable in knowing who might be the best player to take a face-off for certain game conditions.

SPOTTING

Most coaches use game spotters high in the stands or press box. The spotter uses a phone or walkie-talkie system to talk to the bench coach. Sometimes, the head coach goes up high to do the spotting and pass the information on to the bench coach. Bench coaches do not get as good a view as the spotter high above the ice. Spotters are valuable.

STATISTICS

Computers have made statistics easy and quick. There are some good software programs on the market, but a coach can make his or her own with the use of spreadsheets on the computer. With the laptop computers, the stats can be recorded as the game goes on.

SCOUTING

Scouting other teams can be helpful, if the correct information is found. Good scouts look for trends and

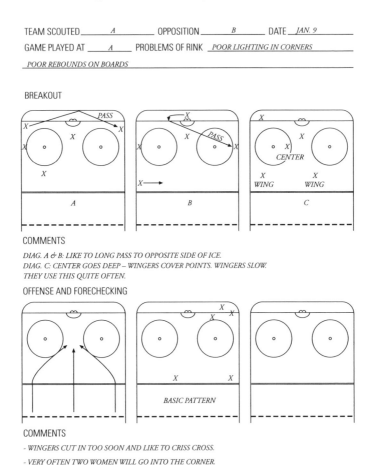

TEAM SCOUTED _____ A _____ OPPOSITION _____ B _____ DATE _JAN. 9_____

GAME PLAYED AT _____ A _____ PROBLEMS OF RINK _POOR LIGHTING IN CORNERS_____

_POOR REBOUNDS ON BOARDS_____

BREAKOUT

COMMENTS

DIAG. A & B: LIKE TO LONG PASS TO OPPOSITE SIDE OF ICE.
DIAG. C: CENTER GOES DEEP – WINGERS COVER POINTS. WINGERS SLOW.
THEY USE THIS QUITE OFTEN.

OFFENSE AND FORECHECKING

COMMENTS

- WINGERS CUT IN TOO SOON AND LIKE TO CRISS CROSS.
- VERY OFTEN TWO WOMEN WILL GO INTO THE CORNER.

Figure 10-3: Scouting Chart

tendencies as well as weaknesses and strengths. It is usually best to have a form or chart to help organize the data and what to look for so that nothing is forgotten (figure 10-3).

Chapter Eleven: Communications

Communications between the coach and players are vital. The following are some guidelines that might be helpful.

THE OBJECTIVE

The objective of what you want to say must be clear and precise. There should be no possibility of misinterpretation. There should be no hidden meanings. Be certain of your message in case you have to defend it.

INFORMATION

Know all the facts — good and bad. When gathering facts, you should be able to answer the who, what, when, where, why and how.

BREVITY

Keep your messages brief. People tend to forget some parts if the message is long. If necessary, break down the message into parts and into sequence. This helps in remembering.

THE TARGET

Target your message to the person responsible for carrying out the message. Be careful when giving the message to someone else in the hope that it will get relayed correctly. Face-to-face messages are best.

KNOW YOUR TARGET

Some players communicate differently than others. Some think differently than others. When you know your target, it is easier to explain the message.

INTEREST

It might not always be possible, but try to keep the message interesting. Salesmen use the term "hook" as a means of grabbing the person's interest or attention. A short statement that grabs the player's attention is a powerful communication technique.

FOLLOW-THROUGH

When a message is given, be sure to follow-through to make sure the request has been done. Do not give a message and forget about it.

PICTURES

Good communicators are able to talk in pictures so that the player gets a good image in her mind of exactly what must be done. The message is in words, but the receiving of the message is in pictures. A good picture is easier to remember.

HOW YOU SAY IT

How you say a message is often more important than the message itself. Be convincing in conveying the message. Show no hesitancy or uncertainty. Speak with energy and vitality. At times, even a smile can help.

OR ELSES

Do not give a message an "or else" statement at the end. Usually, someone will say: "Or else what?" If you do not have an answer, just laugh it off. They got the message.

BODY LANGUAGE

Back up your words with the correct body language. Incorrect body language might alter the meaning of the message.

QUESTIONS

Coaches are often confronted with questions. Some fear these questions. Look upon these questions as an opportunity to present your reasons and clear any misconceptions.

TELEPHONES

Telephones are great, and fast, communicators. Unfortunately, many people cannot convey their message over the phone accurately. They "hummm," "haaa," etc. Get organized and state your message clearly. If leaving a phone number, give it slowly so that the receiver can write the number down. Always repeat the phone number. It is amazing how many people leave a phone number on an answer machine so fast that the message has to be replayed several times to get the number.

MEETINGS

Never have a meeting unless there is an objective to the meeting. Useless meeting are irritating and of no value. They just cause hard feelings. Have your meeting organized and as short as needed. Solve the problem and move on. Do not belabor the problem, as this might create other problems.

SPEECHES

Coaches often have to give speeches to various groups. Some rules are:

1. Do not memorize the speech. Know the sequence of ideas, but talk to the people with a free and easy method.

2. Never ever read the speech. This is boring and uninteresting. Freewheel it.

3. If you use or need notes, highlight the key words and that will trigger what needs to be said. This way, the words will come out more naturally.

4. Use the guidelines previously mentioned. Use brevity and do not belabor a point. If you are good with humor, use it. If not, stay away from

humor. Nothing is worse than someone trying to be funny.

5. When you speak, be natural and human. You are not a statue.

6. Look at the audience. This builds rapport.

7. Do not make distracting noises or moves. No nervous fidgeting, like with change in the pocket. If stuck, do not "hummm" and "haaa." Eliminate the "you knows."

8. Have a good beginning and end. Keep it short in the middle.

Chapter Twelve:
Leadership

Leaders determine the future. Coaches determine the future, which is sometimes good and sometimes bad. Good coaches know their team.

Good coaches have a philosophy. A philosophy gives direction to the players and coach. A philosophy also helps in the decision-making process. Decisions are made according to the philosophy for the team. A consistent philosophy will also make it easier for the players to understand where they are going and what the coach will and will not tolerate. A consistent philosophy will help to eliminate uncertainty in rules, strategy, discipline and team goals.

As part of the philosophy, the coach should be open with his or her players. This might mean listening to ideas on strategy, discipline, etc. The coach might not accept such input, but the coach should at least listen and give the players their say. Good coaches know when to accept and reject such ideas with no feeling of malice toward the player's input. Sometimes, the players have good ideas. A feeling of trust can develop by this type of interaction. Being flexible does not mean the coach has to "give in" or weaken his or her philosophy. The two can be compatible.

Rules are part of the team's and coach's philosophy. Expectations are also part of this philosophy. Rules should be as few as possible. Rules are a form of negative statements. A rule means that maybe the coach cannot trust his or her players, so a rule has to be made. Never have a rule you cannot enforce. If you have a rule, you must enforce it. A rule that is not enforced is of little value and dangerous to the power of the coach. In most cases, it is best to have expectations. The players are expected to do this or to do that. Expectations give the coach some latitude in discipline. Rules do not.

Two of the most valuable assets a coach has are his or her eyes and ears. Good coaches look and listen, are calm and have patience. Looking and listening to the action around him or her makes him or her aware of various situations. So much information is not directed at the coach, as it spreads among the players. Good coaches learn to read the situation through body language, comments and humor. Silence is a good indicator of feelings. Silence after a comment says a lot. Laughter after a comment says a lot. Facial and body movements after a comment say a lot. Learn to read the team through the noise and the silence.

Good coaches are not selfish. They are not carried away with their ego. They give credit to their players, managers and assistants. With a good job done, the coach will get the credit anyway, so there is no need to go looking for applause. Pass the credit and good comments on to the team. They will appreciate it. Some coaches preach team unity, yet they take credit when anything good happens. This is a contradiction. Team unity is sharing the credit. Many coaches take this attitude: "If they had done what I told them, we would have won." Making this statement is trying to protect one's ego. Perhaps better coaching would have made the players do what they were told. Telling players to do something is not coaching. Anyone can tell a player something. Good coaches tell the players and develop the habit in the player so that they will do it. Weak coaches tell their players what to do. Great coaches build habits and change behavior so that the players are able to do what they are told.

There comes a time when a coach must use anger to express true feelings. This should not be overdone or used too often. Too much anger is ignored. Anger should be saved for the appropriate time — when it is really needed. A coach who does not get angry when it is needed might be sending the message that he or she does not really care. When used appropriately, the players know they had it coming and know they deserved it.

Coaches are often concerned with their control of the team. They become afraid of giving responsibility to the players. Giving responsibility to the players does not mean lack of control. The coach still has the team structure and philosophy to guide the responsibility. The players must still act within the expectations of the team and coach.

Many coaches fail to utilize their assistant coaches properly. Each assistant coach must have specific duties. Each assistant must be given his or her assignment as to where on the ice he or she is to be, and what he or she is to look for and coach for each drill, scrimmage and game. Hire good assistants, not just friends. If a good assistant is not available, then don't hire one. Weak assistants are a problem. Be careful of assistants trying to steal your power. Weak assistants and power-hungry assistants should be fired. No questions. Loyalty, dedication and hard work cannot be compromised.

Being decisive is a trait of good coaches. They make decisions as quickly as needed. The decision-making process is not drawn out. If needed, the decision can be corrected later. Indecisive coaches are doomed to failure. Uncertainty in a decision can cause team problems. When a decision is not made, the players will talk about what should and should not be done. This might split the team into sides — for and against. Make the decision, get it over with and move on.

Losses and mental defeats will plague the coach. This goes with the job. Confidence, esteem, worry and depression will occur, but make it short. There is work to do. There are corrections and adjustments to be made. Defeat can be a good teacher. Use it properly. Defeats are only temporary. There can be wonderful happenings in the future.

Chapter Thirteen:
Decision Making

Many decisions must be made at the moment. There is no time for delay or procrastination. Sometimes, the coach has more time for decisions but not as a rule. In most cases, do not drag out a decision. Lack of a decision shows a lack of direction and philosophy. No decision or a delay in a decision might split the team, as the players start deciding what should be done or not done. This creates players going off in various directions and a lack of team unity. If the decision was incorrect, then correct it as quickly as possible.

Information is valuable to decision-making. If possible, make the decision when all the information is in. Gather the information quickly. Only delay a decision when searching for more facts. Never delay a decision in the hope the problem will go away. It won't.

Getting the entire team to accept a decision is not always possible. Players usually accept decisions in how it affects them personally. These are problems, but they can be overcome. If the team has a good philosophy, rules and expectations, then acceptance will usually be understood.

A coach's power will also make the acceptance of a decision easier. Weak coaches will have problems. Winning coaches have an easier time with decision-making, as winning solves a lot of problems. Winning coaches have more power and influence.

DECISION-MAKING STYLES

Decision-making styles span between autocratic and democratic. The situation often determines how much autocratic style is needed and how much democratic style is needed. Especially with larger groups, coaching leans to the autocratic style.

The autocratic-style coach makes all decisions. An advantage of this system is that there is a consistent pattern, as the players soon learn the coach's style. The players have little or no input. Many people do not like this style, but most players accept this as needed. Actually, many players do not want the responsibility of making decisions. They just want to play. Some coaches have tried to let the player select the team, select the game lineup, etc. This system often fails because it takes too many meetings, discussions, etc. Some players could not make a decision involving their friends. Be careful going democratic.

The democratic style ranges from the players making all decisions to some decisions. The players can get the feel that this is their team. They are responsible to the course of play. The democratic process is time-consuming. Team decisions can split the team, as some players might not like other players who voted against their vote. Some players might even start lobbying for favorable votes to their desires. Very often, all the players do not have all the information to make a decision. Just because the group made the decision, it does not mean it is a good decision. A majority vote does not mean a good decision.

The coach will have to decide what style or variations of each style is best for the situation. Some coaches start off very autocratic and then ease into some democracy. The team's personality will often dictate the style. The situation or team personality will determine what style to use for the moment and the season.

Section 5:
Team Strategy
and Skills

Team strategy must fit the personnel. If the players cannot perform or adapt to the desired strategy, then maybe an alternative strategy might be best employed. There are various styles illustrated in this book. A coach might use one or more of these strategies or he or she might even use parts of each to devise his or her own strategy.

Strategy must flow from one stage to the next. A forechecking strategy must coordinate with the backchecking strategy. The backchecking style must coordinate with the defensive strategy and breakout play. The breakout play must move smoothly into attack or offensive style and then be backed up with the forechecking style.

Chapter Fourteen: Basic Team Strategies

The following symbols are the keys to the figures.

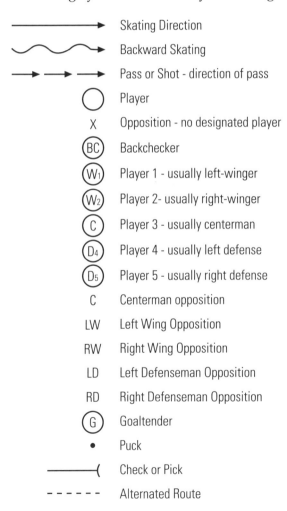

⟶	Skating Direction
∿⟶	Backward Skating
→ → →	Pass or Shot - direction of pass
◯	Player
X	Opposition - no designated player
BC	Backchecker
W₁	Player 1 - usually left-winger
W₂	Player 2- usually right-winger
C	Player 3 - usually centerman
D₄	Player 4 - usually left defense
D₅	Player 5 - usually right defense
C	Centerman opposition
LW	Left Wing Opposition
RW	Right Wing Opposition
LD	Left Defenseman Opposition
RD	Right Defenseman Opposition
G	Goaltender
•	Puck
⟶⊣	Check or Pick
- - - - -	Alternated Route

Hockey strategy breaks down into two basic situations: the 1-on-1 and the 2-on-1. Offensive strategy is trying to set up a 2-on-1 situation to gain an advantage. Defensive strategy is trying to prevent the opponents from gaining a 2-on-1 advantage. All situations are extensions of the 1-on-1 and 2-on-1. The 3-on-1, 3-on-2, 2-on-1 are all variations of the 1-on-1 and the 2-on-1.

DEFENSIVE
One-on-One Defensive

Defensive strategy is based on playing the percentages. It is better to have the opposition shoot from far out than close in or have them shoot from an angle rather than from the slot. In team strategy, we must not forget the goaltender. In defensive play, it is particularly important for the defensewoman and goaltender to coordinate their play so that the goaltender is always able to see the puck and is not screened. If the goaltender knows what her defensewoman is doing, then she is better able to be in position to play the puck. Also, if the forwards know what the goaltender and defensewoman are doing, then they will also know what to do.Figure 14-1 shows the guidelines of the slot that the defensewomen use when backing up to the net.

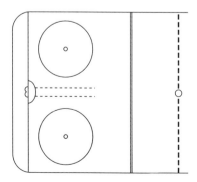

Figure 14-1: Slot Guidelines

Also, the defensewoman should shade to the attackers body so that the goaltender is able to see the puck. The defensewomen's main purpose is to force the attacker to the side and out of the slot. The defensewoman must not lunge at the attacker because if she misses, the attacker has clear access to the goal (figure 14-2).

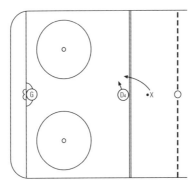

Figure 14-2

If the defensewoman has a backchecker to help her, then the backchecker plays the puck, the defensewoman plays the attackers body, and the goaltender plays the shot. If the goaltender gets the puck, then the backchecker should be ready for a breakout pass from the goalie. The defensewoman must play the attackers body — even after the attacker has taken the shot — so that the attacker has no chance for a rebound or to intercept the pass.

If the puck carrier is approaching from the side, the defensewoman still uses the backup guideline. This keeps the attacker to the side and out of the slot. If the defender moves too close to the boards, then the attacker has a better chance of moving into the slot. By playing the guideline, the defender is also in better position if another attacker enters the picture (figure 14-3).

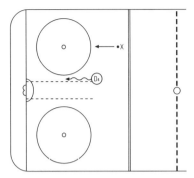

Figure 14-3

Two-on-One Defensive

If the attack is a 2-on-1, the goaltender plays the puck carrier along the boards and the defensewoman plays the other attacker. The defensewoman maintains her position on the backup guidelines but in position to help prevent a pass to the other attacker. The defensewoman's backup should be even with the puck carrier so that the puck carrier cannot cut behind the defensewoman to the goal. As you will notice in figure 14-4, the two attackers are in the low-percentage scoring positions of a bad angle and far out. It is important that the defensewoman does not commit herself and leave one of the attackers clear access to the goal.

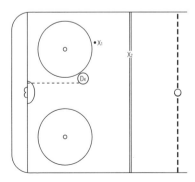

Figure 14-4

The defensewoman should not try to cover both forwards. You cannot be in two places at once. If she tries to cover two players, then she will start rushing here and there, chasing the puck and accomplishing little. The defensewoman usually ends up out of the play, with the two attackers having an easy time.

If the two attackers are coming down the center ice area ,the strategy is much the same. The defensewoman still uses the backup guidelines and tries to force the puck into the weak shooting areas.

Three-on-One Defensive

The 3-on-1 is difficult. Figure 14-5 shows how the defensewoman uses the backup guidelines to keep the puck carrier X1 to the side as well as block a possible pass attempt to X3, who is dangerous because the goaltender has a long move to stop the shot from X3. If the puck carrier passes to X2, then the shot is farther from the net. Also, a shot from X2 means a short move by the goaltender to block the shot. If X2 is the puck carrier, then the goaltender plays the puck carrier and the defensewoman plays the other most dangerous attacker. If there is a backchecker, then she covers X2, the slot or X3, who might actually be the most dangerous attacker, as she is close to the net for a shot or rebound.

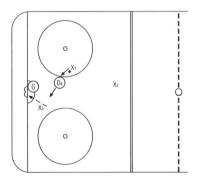

Figure 14-5

Which one the backchecker plays will depend on her position coming back (figure 14-5).

Two-on-Two Defensive

A 2-on-2 is a 1-on-1 with each defender. The puck carrier is forced to the side and out of the slot while the other defender covers the other attacker. A backchecker plays the puck (figure 14-6).

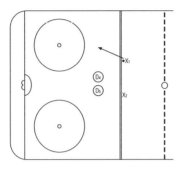

Figure 14-6

One-on-Two Defensive

When two defensewomen have only one attacker, then they can be more aggressive. One defensewoman plays the body while the other plays the puck (figure 14-7).

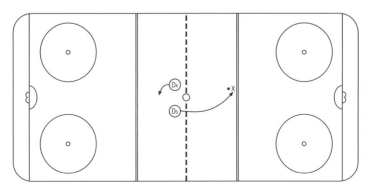

Figure 14-7

Another method for the 1-on-2 is to have the defensewomen move into a tandem position rather than being in the parallel position. A shows what happens in a parallel system when one defensewoman lets the puck carrier get by her. Notice how Ds must chase the puck carrier who has clear access to the net. B, the tandem position, is good because if the attacker beats one defender, then the other defender is in position for coverage of the attacker (figure 14-8).

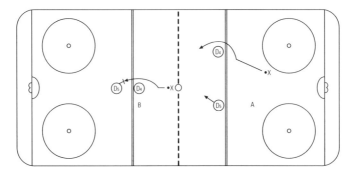

Figure 14-8

Three-on-Two Defensive

If the puck carrier is in the middle of the ice, the defenders try to force the puck to the side for a long shot or poor angle (figure 14-9) when the puck is passed then the players respond as in figure 14-10.

If the puck is to the side, the near defensewoman plays the 2-on-1 while the other defender plays the 1-on-1. The attackers' far winger can be dangerous if she gets the puck because she can have an open net because the goaltender is on the far post playing the puck(figure 14-10).

The backchecker plays the attacker in the slot X2.

A common problem with the 3-on-2 is when the far defensewoman tries to cover two attackers and ends up covering no one. At least take out one player — preferably the most dangerous of the attackers.

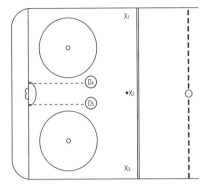

Figure 14-9

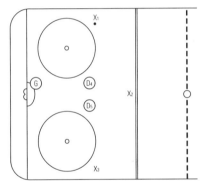

Figure 14-10

OFFENSIVE

One-on-Zero Offensive

This is a breakaway on the goaltender. The best strategy is to make the goaltender move first.

Two-on-Zero Offensive

The best strategy is for the puck carrier to draw the goaltender to the near post. The other attacker drifts to the far side of the goal so that she has the open net to shoot at (figure 14-11).

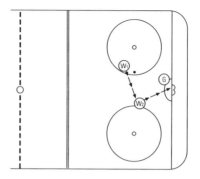

Figure 14-11

One-on-One Offensive

It is often difficult to beat or get around a good defensewoman. The use of fake shots and dekes might be the best and only strategy. Work the defender into a screen-shot position.

Two-on-One Offensive

The winger X1 carries the puck in wide and deep to pull the defender over to her. The puck carrier then cuts to the goal. If her access is blocked, she passes back to her teammate C3 and continues to the goal for a rebound or tip-in (figure 14-12).

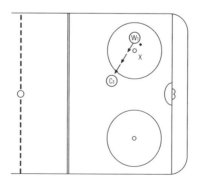

Figure 14-12

If both attackers are approaching the goal from center ice, then they drift to one side and employ the same strategy (figure 14-13).

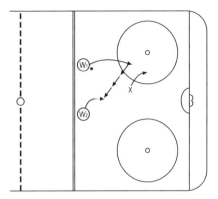

Figure 14-13

A common mistake is for the two attackers to move too close together. This makes it easier for the defender to cover both attackers. As in figure 14-14, both attackers are in a poor shooting angle.

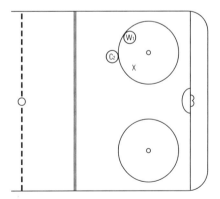

Figure 14-14

Another common mistake on the 2-on-1 is for both attackers lining up in a straight line with the defender. In figure 14-15, notice how W1 has to pass through the defender X to get the puck to W2. If W2 was to move back to the dashed circle, she would be much more dangerous to receive a pass and open up the play.

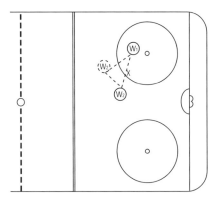

Figure 14-15

Three-on-One Offensive

The best strategy is to get the puck to the far winger, who will have more open net to shoot at because the goaltender will be at the post nearest the puck. The attack sets up like a 2-on-1 to one side, with the far winger drifting in wide and to the goal. Notice the triangulation of the three attackers, which sets up more passing opportunities (figure 14-16).

Two-on-Two Offensive

The two attackers shift to one side to work on one defender rather than both defenders. The 2-on-1 is then used.

If the two attackers are fairly close together, then the puck carrier can cut in front of her teammate and try to pull the defensewoman with her. If the defender moves to the puck carrier, the puck carrier can give a drop pass to her teammate. If the defender does not move with the puck carrier, then the defender can keep the puck (figure 14-17).

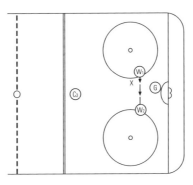

Figure 14-16

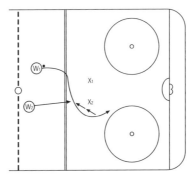

Figure 14-17

Three-on-Two Offensive

The puck goes to the wing and the 2-on-1 is set up with the near defensewoman. The far winger breaks for the net (figure 14-18).

If there is a backchecker on the centerwoman C, the centerwoman breaks to the goal to pull the backchecker in deep to the goal. The far wing now shifts over to the

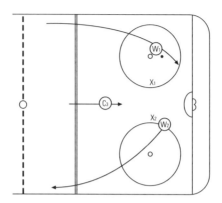

Figure 14-18

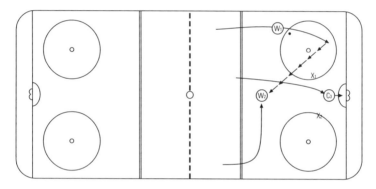

Figure 14-19

slot for a possible pass back from the puck carrier W1. The key to this play is that the far winger W2 must be watching the play develop to see if the centerwoman has a backchecker (figure 14-19).

If the defensewomen are playing too wide, then the centerwoman might have a clear opening to the goal (figure 14-20)

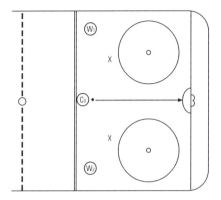

Figure 14-20

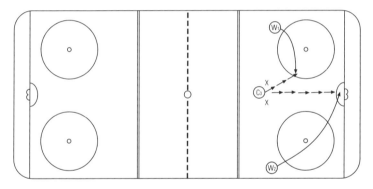

Figure 14-21

If the defensewomen are high and close together and not moving back too fast, then a fast-breaking attacking winger can slip around the defensewomen and take a soft or flip pass from the centerwoman or play for a rebound from the centerwoman's shot on goal (figure 14-21).

Chapter Fifteen:
The Breakout Play

The breakout play usually starts from behind the net. The key to the breakout play is to make sure the team has positive possession of the puck before trying to break out. The players must wait in position until a teammate has positive possession before breaking out. If the players move out too soon, then defensive coverage is lacking (figure 15-1).

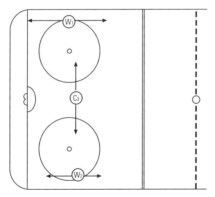

Figure 15-1

Figure 15-1 shows the basic position for the breakout. The wings are wide and the centerwoman is in the center ice area, skating parallel to the blue line. By skating parallel to the blue line, it is easier to take a pass from the defensewoman behind the net. If the centerwoman breaks up the ice too soon, then she has to take the pass looking over her shoulder. Also, it is difficult to hit the centerwoman with a pass while she is skating away from the play. The wingers must also not skate up the

ice too soon. Nothing kills the play more than the forwards moving out too soon.

If the centerwoman is not in the end zone, she should
cross over the blue line close to the boards and then
break parallel to the blue line to receive the pass (figure
15-2).

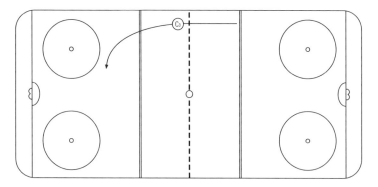

Figure 15-2

If the center ice area is too congested (figure 15-3),
then the centerwoman can go behind the net. When
going behind the net, the centerwoman has the option
of picking up the puck or leaving the puck. The options
depend on the positioning of the forecheckers. If the

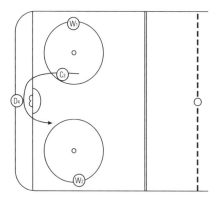

Figure 15-3

area is clear, she can take the puck and proceed up the center lane.

If she takes the puck and is confronted by a forechecker, she can then drop the pass back to her defensewoman so that the play can continue (figure 15-4).

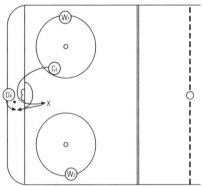

Figure 15-4

If a forechecker is positioned in front of the goal (figure 15-5), the centerwoman can leave the puck with the defensewoman and proceed wide to the corner. The winger on the side of the centerwoman then proceeds to the center ice area to become the centerwoman. The defensewoman can then pass to the centerwoman or winger.

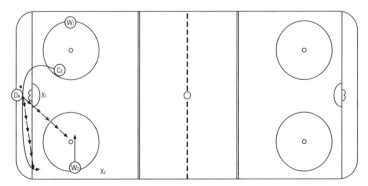

Figure 15-5

The sequence of events is:

1. Do not break out too soon. Wait until everyone is ready.

2. Pass to the centerwoman in the mid-ice area.

3. If the centerwoman goes behind the net, she will take the puck or leave it for the defensewoman.

4. If the centerwoman takes the puck, she breaks up the middle. If interfered with by a checker, she can pass the puck back to the defensewoman.

5. If the centerwoman leaves the puck, she goes wide into the corner while the winger nearest the centerwoman breaks to center ice to become the centerwoman.

Chapter Sixteen:
The Three-Two System

This name comes from the three forwards working as a unit and the two defensewomen working as a unit. This system was hockey's basic system, and it is still used today. Modern hockey has given this system many variations.

DEFENSIVE END ZONE PLAY

Winger in Puck Corner and Center on Near Point

The winger goes into the corner with her defensewoman (figure 16-1). The defensewoman plays the attacker's body, and the winger picks up the puck.

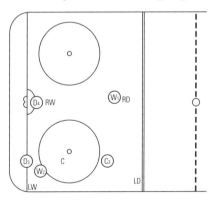

Figure 16-1

The centerwoman covers the near point.

When puck possession is gained, the players move to their breakout positions (figure 16-2).

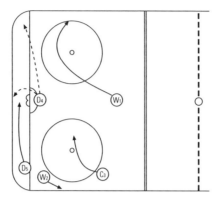

Figure 16-2

Both Wings on the Points

This strategy is similar to the previous formation, except the centerwoman goes into the corner while the winger plays the point (figure 16-3).

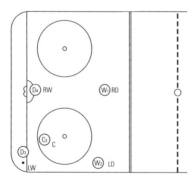

Figure 16-3

First Forward in the Corner and Second Forward on the Point

Same as the above strategies, except the nearest to the puck forward between the winger and center goes into the corner while the other covers the point (figure 16-4).

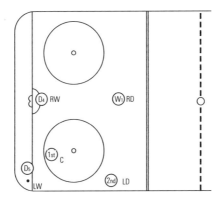

Figure 16-4

One Woman Covering Both Points

This coverage might give weak point coverage but strong coverage low in the slot and corners (figure 16-5).

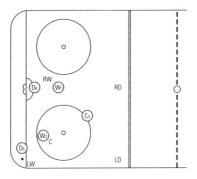

Figure 16-5

OFFENSIVE END ZONE PLAY

Winger in the Corner

The winger plays the corner and the center backs up the winger (figure 16-6). The winger plays the woman, and the center picks up the puck.

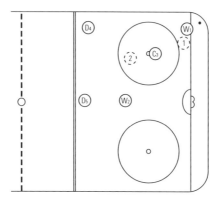

Figure 16-6

Center in the Corner

This is the same strategy as winger in the corner. When the center goes into the corner, the two wings are in position for backchecking duties (figure 16-7).

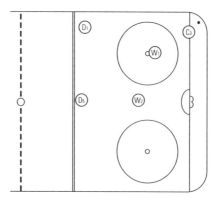

Figure 16-7

First in the Corner, Second Backup

Same strategy again, except the first forward between the center and winger goes into the corner with the other acting as backup (figure 16-8).

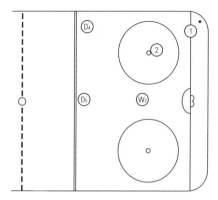

Figure 16-8

Player Movement When the Puck Goes into the Other Corner

With puck movement to the other corner, figure 16-9 shows the rotation. The positioning is similar to that of the original positioning on the previous side.

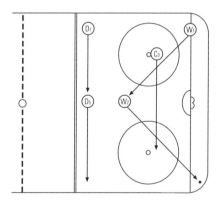

Figure 16-9

If the opposition gains puck control and evades W1, the center or backup woman takes coverage of the puck carrier (figure 16-10).

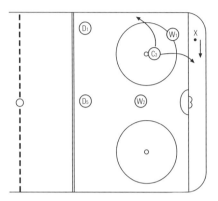

Figure 16-10

If the puck is carried behind the net, player movement is shown in figure16-11.

Notice how the center C3 forces and follows the puck carrier to behind the net but stays in front of the goal as the winger W2 picks up the puck carrier.

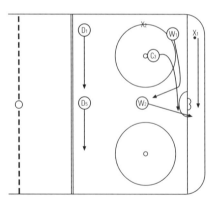

Figure 16-11

If the puck carrier is not stopped (figure 16-12), then the winger W2 keeps swinging around to pick up her check X2. The center — in front of the net — covers the puck carrier, and the other winger picks up her check. The defensewomen shift accordingly.

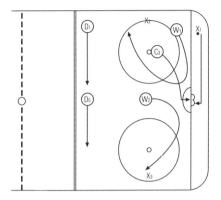

Figure 16-12

This strategy puts the players into position for backchecking duties (figure 16-13).

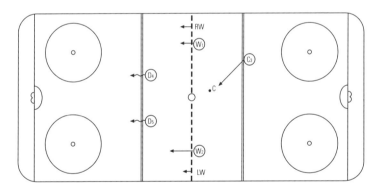

Figure 16-13

FACE-OFF POSITIONS
Defensive End Zone Face-Off
Figure 16-14 shows the basic face-off positions.

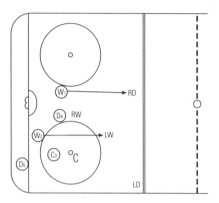

Figure 16-14

Offensive End Zone Face-Off
Figure 16-15 shows the basic formation.

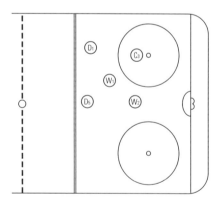

Figure 16-15

PENALTY KILLING – THE BOX FORMATION
Defensive End Zone – One Woman Short

The box formation (figure 16-16) is the basic style. The objective is to keep the puck outside the box and away from the slot.

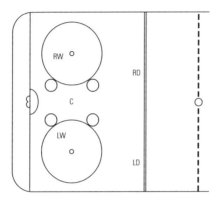

Figure 16-16

The box shifts towards the puck. In figure 16-17, the defensewoman D5 moves towards the puck but does not become too aggressive in the event she does not get the puck. The main concern is to not let the puck carrier get behind the defender and into the slot area.

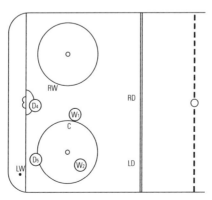

Figure 16-17

If the point woman LD has the puck (figure 16-18), then the box shifts to the puck. W2 must not rush the point woman LD unless she can get the puck. She must not let LD get behind her and into the slot.

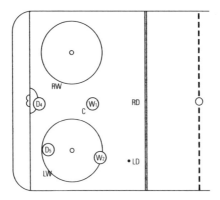

Figure 16-18

If LD passes to RD, the players rotate, as in figure 16-19.

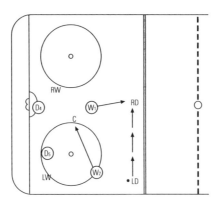

Figure 16-19

Defensive End Zone – Two Women Short

Figure 16-20 shows the basic triangle. C3 has coverage of both points.

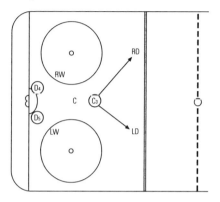

Figure 16-20

Figure 16-21 shows the tandem positioning. The nearest player to the puck carrier moves out to check this person.

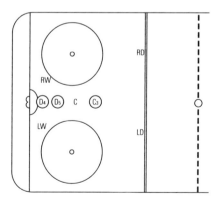

Figure 16-21

Forechecking – One Woman Short

The first forechecker plays the puck carrier. If the puck carrier goes behind the goal (figure 16-22), the forechecker stays in front of the net. If she goes behind the goal, she might get trapped and be unable to backcheck. The second forward lines up in tandem with the first forechecker. As the opposition breaks out, the two forcheckers peel off to backcheck the wings.

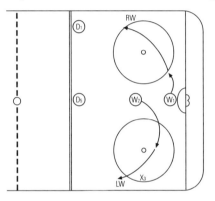

Figure 16-22

Some strategies simply have the two forecheckers cover their wings tightly and let the opposition break out. This strategy prevents a forechecker from getting caught or trapped in the far end of the ice.

THE POWER PLAY

Defensive End Zone

The break out play is basically the same as previously discussed. It can be advantageous to have the defensewoman in front of the goal swing over and rush up the ice with a winger (figure 16-23). This rush gives the attack two wingers to one side for a strong side and an attacking player advantage.

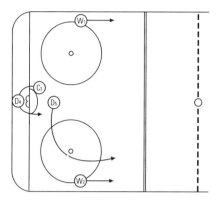

Figure 16-23

Another effective play is to have the center delay her
return and then cut parallel to the blue line to receive a
long pass for the breakout. This play can trap a
forechecker deep into the end zone (figure 16-24).

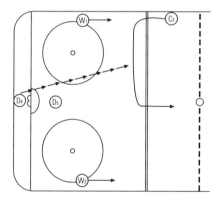

Figure 16-24

Offensive End Zone

Figure 16-25 shows the basic team formation.

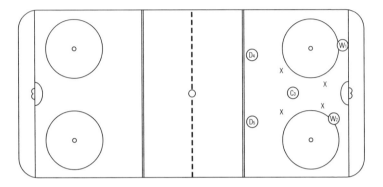

Figure 16-25

Chapter Seventeen: The Box Strategies

The box strategies have the players playing a box formation with an extra woman.

THE TWO-ONE-TWO BOX

This might also be called the five-woman box. Figure 17-1 shows the checking responsibilities. Notice how the wingers and defensewomen check each other. This makes sense, as these two meet in the corners at the defensive end and at the point in the attacking end. Basketball also uses this checking system.

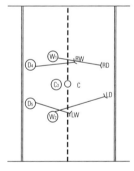

Figure 17-1

The key to the box is that the centerwoman maintains a triangle with her defensewomen in each end of the rink (figure 17-2). The center C3 is half-defensewoman and half-forward. This triangle gives strong defensive coverage. The two wingers are free to roam and attack quickly. It is imperative for defenders to stay between their check and the net.

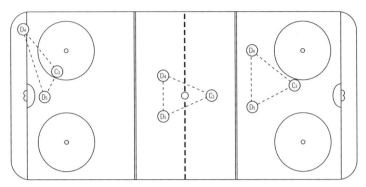

Figure 17-2

Figure 17-3 shows the formation in the defensive end.

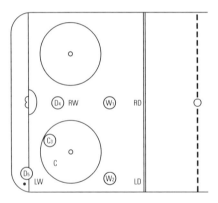

Figure 17-3

Figure 17-4 shows the areas of responsibility for each player. The center C3 backs up each square as needed. The defensewoman's responsibility is to contain the attacking puck carrier RW in the corner. In the corner, she is not dangerous if all her teammates are covered. The defensewoman D4 must not rush the puck carrier carelessly because if she misses, she is trapped in the corner while the puck carrier is now out of the corner and is dangerous.

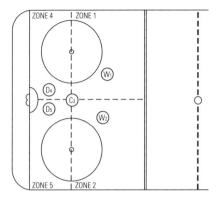

Figure 17-4

Figure 17-5 shows the formation when the puck is in the defensive corner. When the puck goes into the other corner, the players just maintain formation and shift over to the other side.

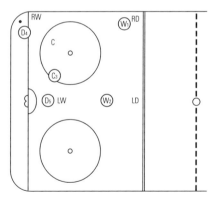

Figure 17-5

Figure 17-6 shows the formation in the attacking end.

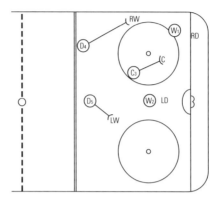

Figure 17-6

If the opposition breaks out in a three-woman rush (figure 17-7), the center and both defensewomen maintain their triangle and checks.

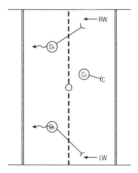

Figure 17-7

BREAKOUT PLAYS

The following Figures illustrate various breakout plays. As you will notice, the players are already in breakout formation. The passing plays are endless (figures 17-8 through 17-16).

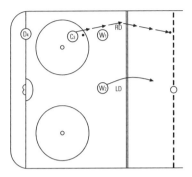

Figure 17-8

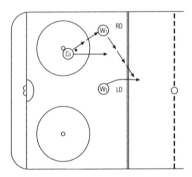

Figure 17-9

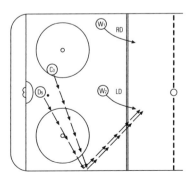

Figure 17-10

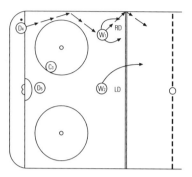

Figure 17-11

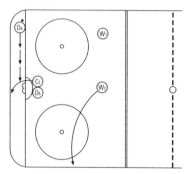

Figure 17-12

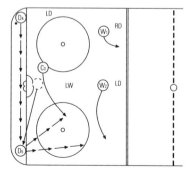

Figure 17-13

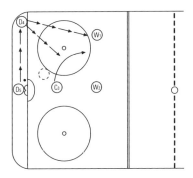

Figure 17-14

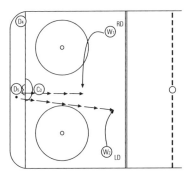

Figure 17-15

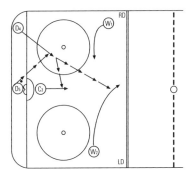

Figure 17-16

ATTACKING PLAYS

From the breakout, the team is on the attack. The defensewomen and center still maintain their triangulation and back up the forwards. The positioning of the wings will depend on how they break out (figure 17-17). They play to the advantage.

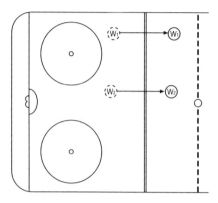

Figure 17-17

If the two forwards break out together, they can do the 2-on-1, as in figure 17-18.

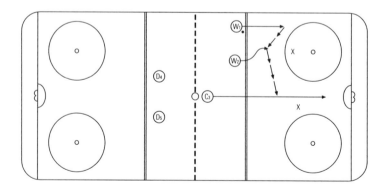

Figure 17-18

If the W1 forward continues wide and deep, she has many options for passes, as in Figure 17-19.

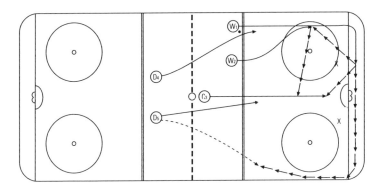

Figure 17-19

If W2 has the puck, then her options are in figure 17-20.

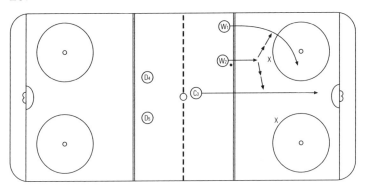

Figure 17-20

FORECHECKING

Forechecking is simple, as the defensewomen and center still maintain their triangle. The wings roam to the situation. Figure 17-21 shows the basic formation.

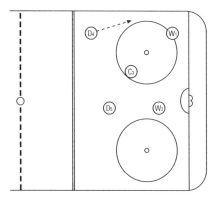

Figure 17-21

Figure 17-22 shows the shifting pattern when the puck goes to the other corner.

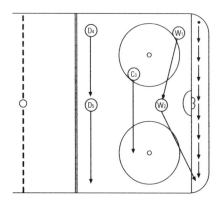

Figure 17-22

BACKCHECKING

When the opposition breaks out, the defenders D4, D5 and C3 maintain their triangle. They force the play to the side, as in Figure 17-23, and the center in the middle can help by playing the slot.

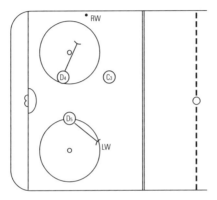

Figure 17-23

If the attacker dumps the puck into the corner, the center breaks into the corner to get the puck while defensewomen maintain their checks (figure 17-24).

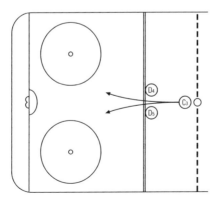

Figure 17-24

FACE-OFFS IN THE DEFENSIVE END ZONE

Figure 17-25 shows the basic face-off formation. Each player checks her regular 2-1-2 check. Notice how W2 is back to take the face-off pass if C-3 gets the draw.

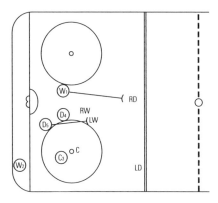

Figure 17-25

FACE-OFFS IN THE OFFENSIVE END ZONE

Figure 17-26 shows the basic formation.

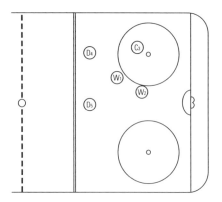

Figure 17-26

Figure 17-27 gives an alternative formation.

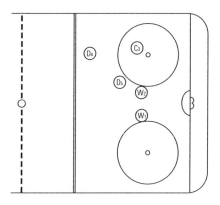

Figure 17-27

PULLED GOALIE FACE-OFF

With only a few seconds left in the game or period, it can be a good idea to pull the goalie and use the extra attacker in the following formations (figure 17-28 and figure 17-29).

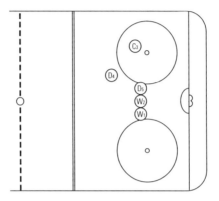

Figure 17-28

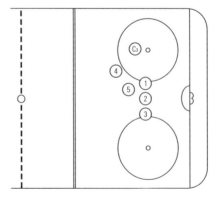

Figure 17-29

PENALTY KILLING

The "Y" Formation for One-Woman Short Forechecking

Again, the defensewomen and center maintain their triangle (figure 17-30). The forward W1 goes to the front of the net and attacks the breakout play. If the breakout moves out, the forward W1 picks up a winger to backcheck.

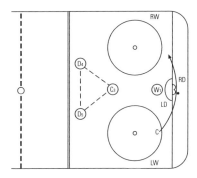

Figure 17-30

Defensive End Zone Play for One-Woman Short

The defensewomen and the center maintain their triangle. The forward W1 covers both points (figure 17-31).

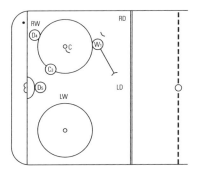

Figure 17-31

PENALTY KILLING FOR TWO-WOMEN SHORT

Forechecking

Forechecking is the basic triangle, with the defensewomen and center (figure 17-32).

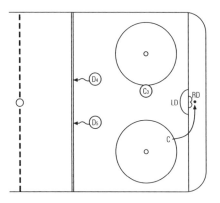

Figure 17-32

Defensive End Zone

Figure 17-33 shows the positioning.

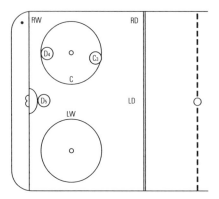

Figure 17-33

A hockey team should not neglect its breakout play, even when playing short-handed. Taking advantage of such an opportunity can often result in a goal.

THE POWER PLAY

The Power Play Breakout

The breakout play as discussed in Chapter 15 will work with the 2-1-2 system.

The Power Play Attack

The breakout play gives a strong side to the attack. A pass to the weak side can be effective, as the opposition might be overemphasizing the strong side (figure 17-34).

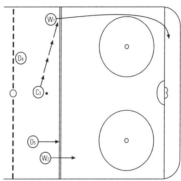

Figure 17-34

Figures 17-35, 17-36, 17-37 and 17-38 show possible plays to the strong side.

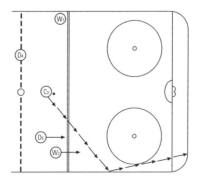

Figure 17-35

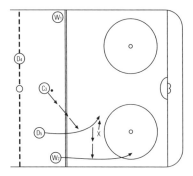

Figure 17-36

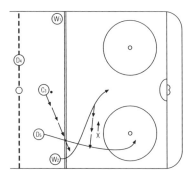

Figure 17-37

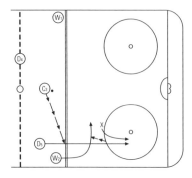

Figure 17-38

When the attackers set up in the end zone, the following formation can be used (figure 17-39).

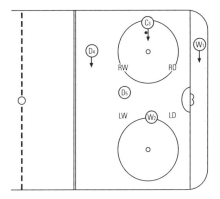

Figure 17-39

Pick plays are highly effective. Figure 17-40 shows the pick from the side.

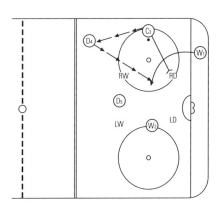

Figure 17-40

The pick can also go the other way, as in Figure 17-41.

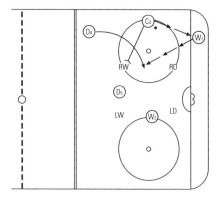

Figure 17-41

The pick can also come from the center area with the defensewomen (figure 17-42).

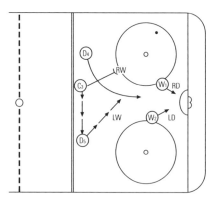

Figure 17-42

Another variation to the power play offensive formation is in figure 17-43. This formation is good for overloading the slot.

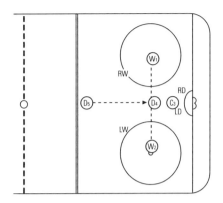

Figure 17-43

Chapter Eighteen:
Other Strategies

THE 1-2-2 SYSTEM

In this strategy, the center C3 (figure 18-1) is moved up in front of her two forwards. In the defensive end, this moves the two forwards a little deeper for protection as well as moving the center up for a quick breakout.

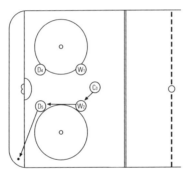

Figure 18-1

When the puck is in the corner, the players just shift to maintain a box in front of the net (figure 18-2).

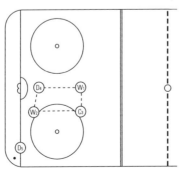

Figure 18-2

When forechecking, the center is the first player into the corner or on the opposition while the other two forwards back her up.

THE 2-2-1 SYSTEM

In this system (figure 18-3), the center C3 is moved back from the box. C3 becomes a defensive player while the other four players are given more freedom for the attack. C3 is also in position to be the first back into her defensive end zone to pick up the puck in the corner or to help the goalie defend. In the offensive end zone, the defensewomen penetrate a little deeper because C3 is there for backup.

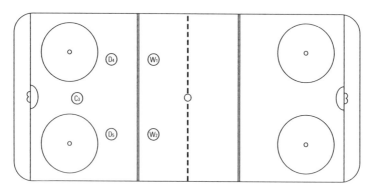

Figure 18-3

WINGER ON WINGER

Winger on winger can be an effective strategy if the opposition has strong wings. The main role of the wingers is to cover the opposition's wings under all circumstances. They are defensive players. This strategy is valuable if you have strong defensive players but are of lesser offensive ability. The winger simply keeps her body between the goal and the player she is defending. The wingers have no complicated strategy. No matter where the puck is, the winger stays on the winger.

Conclusion

From all the strategies in this book, it must be remembered that the best strategies are often the simplest to execute. By simplest, we mean effectively simple to the level of the players. A complex strategy is of little value if it is not executed perfectly. The best way to start development is to go very basic and progress to the desired complexity needed for the group. Do not rush the process. Make sure the learning is permanent before moving on to the more complex level.

Remember: *A simple strategy executed pefectly is more effective, especially under pressure, than a complex strategy not executed perfectly.*

The modern coach must be more versed in the mental aspects of sports psychology, physiology or exercise science of the body, nutrition, and sociology and psychology of the group and individual, decision-making, leadership and management. One book cannot cover all these areas in depth. The coach must read and study these areas.

It is the intent of this book to open up these areas. The coach must read and study books, articles, lectures and seminars in these areas. There is so much to learn. The modern coach is a scientist — studying, experimenting, and researching for more and better ways to serve the team and players. Knowledge is the essence of coaching. The boot camp drill sergeant coach is fading from the scene. The knowledgeable coach is replacing the old style.